QUIET
MOMENTS

Anna J West

Pen Press

First published in Great Britain by Pen Press

All paper used in the printing of this book has been made from
wood grown in managed, sustainable forests.

ISBN13: 978-1-78003-584-0

Printed and bound in the UK
Pen Press is an imprint of
Indepenpress Publishing Limited
25 Eastern Place
Brighton
BN2 1GJ

A catalogue record of this book is available from
the British Library

For all of those who have been in this place.

And…

For Martin, whom I can never thank enough.

With love

CHAPTER ONE

The phone shrilled out its uninvited ring, breaking the Sunday morning silence.

'Phone!' shouted my eldest from the depths of her room. Obviously, I thought as I snuggled further down under the covers, ignoring her call. I begrudged leaving my bed. This was one of the rare Sundays when I had absolutely nothing to do. My plans involved coffee, croissants, a pile of newspapers, their supplements and nothing more, or so I thought. I allowed a contented sigh to pass my lips.

The persistent ring of the phone continued jabbing at my peace of mind with its persecuting demand for attention. The feather-filled duvet muffled the outside world whilst I continued my pursuit of solitude but reality still lurked outside my safe haven. Justification of my thoughts found a gap to sneak in. *It's never for me anyway; well, hardly ever.* My thought process was logical; when you have two teenage daughters the phone is never for you unless it's telesales, or your mum.

'Oh, for God's sake! Am I the only person in this house who knows how to answer the phone?' Scrabbling from my bed, I threw back the quilt, exposing my agitated self to the brightness of the morning. Sheets of scattered newspaper flew high in the air.

'Hello?' I knew I sounded impatient and edgy.

'Anna?' Mum's croaky voice squeezed its way into my unreceptive brain, a totally unwelcome intruder. Great; the last thing I needed was a long drawn out conversation which consisted of nothing but gossip and her unquestionable opinion, which in eyes is always right. I slumped down on the edge of the mattress, feeling its warmth ebb away.

'Hello, Mum.' I hoped I didn't sound as pissed off as I felt, though why I shouldn't, who knows? I watched the last sheet of newspaper glide gently to the floor like an unstrung kite that had lost the breeze. It landed with a hushed rustle softly amongst the jumble of others. I took a deep sigh. It took determination to drag my wandering thoughts back to the conversation in hand.

'Sorry, Mum, you were saying?'

'My sister's dead.'

I fell silent as a brief wave of guilt flooded over me. 'Oh, which one?' I asked. Here was I, cross with her intrusion into my perfect morning of solitude and space, when she had just lost her sister. What kind of daughter was I?

'Joan, Joan in Nottingham.'

Nottingham. I hesitated. That very word churned my stomach into a million tiny knots, wringing out trapped emotion hidden in the depths within the pit of my being, because Nottingham was the place where it all began.

'Anna, are you still there?' The stinging sharpness of her voice held such a contrast to its original sorrowful tone.

'I'm sorry, Mum. You OK?'

'Yes, yes.' Her 'woe is me' voice returned, dull and lifeless, to drone on.

The guilt was gone. This is the point where some of you might think that I sound harsh. Although I know the story for all it is, for a brief moment even I wondered if she deserved more compassion than I lent her, but no. I encourage you to hold judgment until you read on.

The clouds were set over the last day of the sunny spring weekend.

That evening was no different from any other. All of us – that's me, Martin my husband and our two daughters

Elizabeth and Sarah – sat in the lounge. It's a bit of a weekend ritual really. The week flies by with us all pulling in different directions to our own separate destinations; we clatter along disjointedly, hectically and noisily until Sunday comes, then a natural hush seems to fall. A lazy morning and late start replaces my shouts of '*Hurry up, you'll miss the bus; don't expect me to take you into college,*' or '*You can explain to the teacher that you were too lazy to get up on time and that's why you are late.*'

That evening we were watching TV when an advert came on for the NSPCC, an appeal to help stop child abuse. It flitted from one picture to another showing distressed children, but one held my attention wiping all the others into oblivion. The child was standing in a cot, holding on to the bars, staring out into the darkness of an empty room; they were unkempt; their tearstained face portrayed their fear and bewilderment. A sharp stinging behind my eyes forced me to screw my lids shut to stop the tears from falling. A lump rose in my throat, threatening to choke me unless I let it escape as a sob. I managed to contain it. Vivid pictures tumbled through my mind. An uncontrollable avalanche of flashbacks from when I was young, detonated by the scenes being paraded before me, forcing me back in time.

It was dark, very dark. I must have been less than two years old. I was standing in my cot peering through the bars. My voice was hoarse from screaming. I vaguely recall a chink of light appeared as the door was opened. The face of a man turned to look back at me. The light disappeared as he left the room, leaving me alone. I don't know who the man was, or why I was screaming as he left. What I do know is somewhere deep inside this persistent memory makes me feel sick with fear.

Elizabeth's voice cut through my thoughts, jerking me thankfully back into the present.

'Their parents must be sick, they should be locked up. How anyone can hurt an innocent child, I will never know.'

She snuggled up beside me. Looking at her I saw at sixteen she was nearly a woman, her whole life ahead of her. I wrapped my arm around her in a protective hug. Inhaling the smell of mango, I planted a kiss on her freshly washed hair.

'Yes, I know what you mean,' I croaked, forcing my voice through the tightness clutching my throat.

'Don't cry, Mum.' Her voice was full of concern, too wise for her age.

Tilting her face to meet mine, I saw a frown etching a map of unnatural lines across her young forehead. I hugged her tighter. Both our girls know I had what they class as a weird upbringing. I let out snippets sometimes, not too much, not enough to break their bond, though it is shallow, with my mother. It wouldn't be fair. They have the right to make up their own minds and draw their own conclusions. As they grow older they are forming their own opinion of their grandmother's actions and mannerisms.

Oblivious to the full reason I was so emotional, she snuggled in closer. 'It's a good thing that we can help these kids,' she continued. I smiled. Glancing up I caught Martin's eye. He shot me a reassuring look; his silent promise of *I'm here* travelled between us. He is one of the few people who know why, though in my forties, I am still afraid of the dark.

That night brought me a nightmare, a recollection of an incident from when I was two, or maybe three years old.

I was playing in the street where we lived, Simpkin Street. It was a road full of twitching lace curtains and red painted steps. Families tried to make the best of their dismal surroundings. This was still very much a post-war survival area. Row upon row of houses stood like crooked teeth, stained, cracked and ill-repaired. There were even some gaps where buildings were missing leaving their gardens deserted, thanks to 'Hitler's merry men' and their misguided missiles.

We lived in a house just like all the others, a two-up two-down terrace that was built around the turn of the twentieth century, its crumbling, soot-covered brick face squashed as it jostled for room against the steep pavement that lined the narrow tarmac road. From dawn till dusk hordes of children were on the streets. They ran on the bombsites, played in the derelict ruins and built their imaginary worlds. The girls kicked off their shoes to play hopscotch, unashamedly revealing the patchwork of darns in their socks. Mothers wearing aprons, some with curlers in their hair, stood on their front step and shouted, 'Clear off!' to the boys who sported short back and sides and short trousers to match, as they kicked footballs against house walls.

The women stayed at home to cook and clean and look after the armies of small children whilst the men worked in factories, or the mines. No stiff upper lips here; just hard graft. Friday nights the men shaved and slicked Brylcreem on their hair before going to the pub, returning late in full voice, singing long-remembered songs learned from their fathers before them. The women's embarrassed hushing whispers could be heard the length of the street, as they ordered their men folk to 'Shush, there's children sleeping.' This inevitably was followed by the crashing sound of tumbling milk bottles, male giggles, and the hurried muffled slam of front doors closing. I often lay awake and listened to those sounds; it was comforting to know there were others around.

The day my nightmare took me back to was a warm sunny one. I was sitting on the step tapping the heels of my scuffed shoes against the pavement. I watched the other children play. One spoke.

'Our mums says we're not to play with you, that you don't get no dinner, that your dad's a lazy bastard.'

I didn't reply. I was used to these taunts. The kids were never brave enough to come near the step so I knew I was safe. I hummed to drown out what he was saying. One by one the others joined in, chanting and yelling, calling me names like 'bastard child' and 'tart's kid'. Most of the words I didn't, and I'm sure they didn't, know the meaning of.

Putting my fingers in my ears I hummed a little louder; I didn't want to hear. I shut my eyes; I didn't want to see. I sat there for what seemed like forever. The taunts subsided to sniggers and whispers. I heard footsteps running away, and then silence. A small sigh of relief escaped from my lips and blew soft reassuring air onto my bare wrists. I removed my fingers from my ears and let my body relax. Safe at last, but I was wrong.

I suppose because they had taunted me for so long without any repercussion they got a little braver. Opening my eyes I saw the boy who had started the shouting was coming towards me with a dinner fork.

''Ere little poor girl, want some dinner?' He was waving something in front of me, I sat still, terror cementing my small frame to the concrete step, scared to move or to run indoors, knowing my dad was much worse to face than this.

'Come on, little girl – eat up.'

Suddenly the boy was on top of me, stabbing the fork into my face, trying to make me eat the struggling worm impaled on the end of it. I backed away as far as I could, pressing my backbone tight against the closed front door. I screamed as the cold writhing body touched my cheek. This allowed the boy enough room to push the worm into my open mouth. Throwing the fork, he slammed my jaw shut.

'Chew, chew,' he taunted.

His grubby fingers bit into my face. The pressure of his hand forced my mouth up and down, slamming my teeth

6

together hard. I had no choice but to chew the fleshy contents into a gritty pulp. A mixture of fluid and mush leaked out of the corners of my lips and trickled down onto my chin. As I looked into his eyes I saw the same evil glint I saw so often in my dad's, coupled with the reflection of my own pathetic face.

As suddenly as it all started it was over, he let go and ran off with the others, laughing as they went. I spat out what was left of the worm, clearing my mouth with my fingers, trying to rid myself of the rancid taste and dirt, choking until I was sick.

I woke with Martin gently shaking me.

'Hey, you were having a dream. You OK?' He had put the bedside lamp on. The room flooded with a welcome glow chasing away the demons that hid in the dark corners of my mind. I looked up at his concerned face. No more was said, he just held me.

I lay there until the soft regular rhythm of his breathing told me he had gone back to sleep. Then I crept from the bed. I could still taste the dirt of my dream in my mouth. I went to the bathroom, vomited, cleaned my teeth and returned to the warmth and safety of Martin's arms.

CHAPTER TWO

Most people think it's great to have a good memory, but that depends on what your memories are. Mine, as you are already aware, start from early childhood. Other people try to look back this far in their minds, and struggle to place the facts. The hazy mist that divides truth from fantasy, fact from fiction, makes it nearly impossible for them to recall the past from the maze in which it hides. With me the mist does not exist. The maze is a straight path. The past reappears all too readily with crystal clarity, uninvited, and at the least expected moment.

I was born in 1960, second live child to my mum and dad. I say 'live' because Mum is very secretive about any previous, or later, pregnancies. I know she definitely gave birth to more children both before and after me, but it seems on the rare occasions I get her to talk, the numbers change. There were other pregnancies too ending in the form of miscarriage, or of back street or self-inflicted abortions.

The first born to my parents was a boy, Amon, named after Dad's brother. I find this ridiculous, as Dad and his brother didn't really get on and saw very little of each other. Why on earth would my parents want to name their child after someone they didn't particularly like? It would only make sense if they thought they would get something out of it. I have no doubt that this absurdity was for no other reason than that. Most things my parents did were for self-gain or show. These types of actions were always instigated by Dad, though I have to say it seems Mum readily followed his example.

Mum has always said she can't remember when Amon was born, when he died or even where he was buried. I find this hard to believe. I made one phone call to the local registry office, which helped me find out all the information I wanted to know. He was born on Christmas Day 1958, and he died aged just ten minutes old. Cause of death was premature birth. Further investigations revealed Amon was buried in a communal grave in the Nottingham area. The cemetery's apt name for where he is buried is 'Babies Common'. The hospital arranged for disposal of his body. No one attended the funeral because there wasn't one. I don't know if her denial of this and other similar events is for self-preservation, or to cover the fact that she actually cared or cares very little about this or similar incidents and looks on them with her disjointed attitude as part of life, and that's that!

A little under two years later, I came along. Of course I don't remember much of the first few years of my life. The episode I wrote of, prompted by the advert, may or may not be connected to the fact that when I was around 18 months old, my parents took in a lodger. I don't remember his name; I just recall he was Scottish. Mum and Dad went out so he was sometimes left alone with me. I won't say he was asked to babysit because the chances are they would have gone out if he wasn't there anyway. According to people I have spoken with whilst researching for this book, the lodger moved out of our house when he was put in prison for interfering with young children. Though I know some very nice Scottish people, my stomach still tenses when I hear the accent.

My first true recollections begin around 1963 whilst living at Simpkin Street. It was one of the poorest areas in Nottingham. I lived with my mum, dad and six-month-old brother Carl. Our house looked the same as everyone else's. Our lace curtains hung crisply starched and white, cloaking the box sash windows; the step was painted a fiery red, but it was all for show. Open the door, and it was a very different story. Inside, locked away from the world, the house safely held its own secrets.

Downstairs was a front room, sparsely furnished with a sagging brown sofa and matching armchair. Both were stuffed with horsehair, both chafed the back of my legs with their harsh rough covering. In one corner of the room stood a push-button, black and white TV; this had a grey metal box bolted to the side, where we had to post coins in to give us viewing time. Dad would put the coins in only to bust the box open the next day and take them out again. Inevitably, eventually the telly rental man would find out and take it away. He would be let in the house by Mum, whilst Dad, like the coward he was, hid upstairs, too frightened to face the wrath. Mum would apologise and make pathetic unbelievable excuses, pulling me to her, saying how she could not leave her little ones to starve. The man would take the telly from its place muttering about how dishonest people were, and how he had a living to make. A few days later another telly would appear and sit in the corner for a while before being rented to someone honest, someone who deserved it.

Give him his due, Dad was consistent in some things, smoking for instance. His fags were always more important than clothes, or food for that matter. The habit of smoking 40-plus per day remained with him until he died. Many a day he would lounge in the chair puffing away on his Player's No. 10s whilst we sat and watched, our tummies rumbling. I remember thinking maybe smoking stopped you feeling hungry, but found out that wasn't true after stealing a fag from his pack and lighting it from the coal fire. I choked as the smoke invaded my three-year-old lungs, quickly put the fag out and posted the evidence down between the floorboards. How dangerous was that! I don't think Dad ever found out, and I am sure I would have known if he had.

The only other item of furniture in the front room was a large bow-fronted sideboard, which contained a few pieces of linen and china. The floor was covered with cold lino, its faded flowery pattern littered with wear patches, which in places had developed into holes, allowing the floorboards below to peep through. A heavily patterned rug, adorned with tiny burn holes from where the rarely lit fire spattered its extensive debris, lay in front of the fireplace. That was the room that held my first vivid memory of my father's sadistic behaviour.

The only other room downstairs was the kitchen. It housed a large stone sink, a table and three chairs. In the corner was a stand-alone cupboard, made from wood covered in blue Formica. The cupboard was graced with two frosted glass sliding doors at the top where Mum kept her crockery, a drop-down leaf in the middle that served as a work surface, and two doors at the bottom, behind which the pots and pans were kept. There were two doors in the kitchen; one led you up the bare wooden stairs to two bedrooms, and the other to a shared back yard. On blowy days, Mum hung out the washing to flap in the breeze; I remember sitting on the back step watching her. Dad had made a makeshift line from a length of hairy string, its inadequacy showed by the many repair knots that held it together. In the yard was a coal shed where our tin bath hung on the back of the door. In another small shed, cold amongst the cobwebs, nestled the toilet; next to it, suspended from a rusty nail, hung roughly torn squares of newspaper.

The main bedroom was where Mum and Dad slept on a metal-framed bed topped by a lumpy mattress, covered by a washed-out candlewick bedspread. My brother Carl and I shared the other room. I had a single bed covered with a woollen blanket, and he a cot. There was no mattress in the cot, so a drawer had been taken from the large chest that stood in the corner, and placed inside to act as a bed.

We were poor, poorer than most. This was mostly due to the fact that Dad was lazy. At first he insisted that he was ill. He visited the doctor regularly with a string of complaints about various illnesses he was sure he had, but then stopped going when the doctor got fed up with his malingering and refused to give him pills or sign him off sick. From then on he sat in his chair, chain smoking, drinking endless cups of tea and barking orders at Mum. The only times he would leave this position would be to sign for the dole, or if poverty (meaning the lack of money to buy fags, and then only if every avenue of borrowing had been exhausted) forced him to search for work. He would always find a job quite easily, but after only a few short days, or, if we were lucky, weeks, his ill health, hypochondria or 'lazyitis', whatever you want to call it, would entice him to return to his chair, to be waited on hand and foot. He used to say it was never his fault he lost the job.

Occasionally Dad would decide we all needed exercise. Ironic, isn't it? But there you are. I didn't understand him, so I don't expect you to. On these occasions he would say, 'Let's go for a stroll.' Sometimes the stroll would be a few miles, sometimes ten or more. Occasionally I loved the walks we went on. Dad would hold my hand. As we walked he would point things out. Together we would watch birds fly from trees, kneel in hedgerows to pick wild flowers. When the season was right we would pick ripe blackberries from the laden briars, biting into the juicy flesh and then laughing as we poked out our stained tongues.

Other times the walks were living nightmares. If Dad was in one of his moods we would walk until my feet blistered; he would laugh at how pathetic I was and tell me to keep up. I learned from an early age not to complain.

When I was three, Dad went through a stage where he wanted me out of the way as much as possible so he could have Mum's undivided attention. I would be sent outside from early morning till sundown. I was not allowed out of sight, which I guess shows some form of caring, or maybe just more control? Most of my time was spent sitting out front, on the steep concrete step that joined our house directly to the pavement, watching others of my age let their souls dance in the sun, too young for inhibitions, their play carefree. I used to play my own game. If I sat far enough back on the step, perched on my hands to give me height, I could hold my legs out straight, parallel to the step, then bending at the knee bounce my heels down against the step face, and use my skinny muscle-padded calves as a springboard to thrust them back up to horizontal again. I was a lonesome child, so this was a regular pastime.

Bullying was a regular occurrence in my life, both inside and outside home. With my ill-fitting clothes and scrawny appearance, I was a sitting target for the kids outside. That was until the time David moved to our area.

Mum and Dad got friendly with David's parents. David was my hero and though he was a few months younger he was taller and stronger than me. He frightened off the bullies, threatening to hit anyone who called me names. We would sit on the step together holding hands. His sky blue eyes held my gaze as he said, 'I'll look after you; my dad taught me how to punch.' With this he would hold his scrunched-up hand toward me, offering proof of his power. I adored him with childlike awe. Once we saw my mum and David's dad round the back of our coal shed kissing. Their bodies entwined, and their lips pushed together. The sight fascinated us, but they saw us watching them, and David's dad chased us up the garden calling us 'Bloody little buggers' and throwing stones at us. From then on David and I held that special secret.

13

The other kids started to ask us to join in with their games. David would, but I was not allowed. I envied them all.

One day I was sitting alone, in my usual place, on the step, brooding as I watched David play with the other kids. It's funny how we all look back on those golden summer days, and the way we always remember them being so much hotter than nowadays, but that day really was. It was so hot, the road became awash with little volcanic eruptions. I watched fascinated as the hot tarmac swelled into black shiny domes, which then burst, a loud popping sound marking their death. Tiny droplets scattered dancing into the air before they fell and joined the rest of the deflated remains, in pools of sticky black. I wished I could join other kids as they all raced to be the first to pop the ever-rising bubbles, playfully pushing each other out of the way, falling and laughing. But I knew I was not to play with them or leave the step. Dad always kept me away from them; he said he did not want them knowing our business. Years on, with an understanding of what went on, I am not surprised. Back then I knew from experience that I did what Dad said.

Mum would kneel down to my height and say, 'Try to be good.' I still recall the anxious look in her tired eyes, searching my face and watching for my eager nod of agreement. I tried to be good, I tried my hardest, but it rarely seemed that I was good enough. Something I did always upset Dad and I always ended up being in the wrong. Dad always blamed me when things went wrong; Mum usually agreed with him. Her soft look would change to one of a cold and distant carelessness. Why? I didn't know.

Anyway, back to that particular day. One of the girls, a tall gangly child with long matted blonde hair, kept glancing my way. Eventually she stood up from her game and came over to me.

'Wanna go?' she asked, holding out the lolly stick she had been using as her tar bubble-stabbing weapon, towards me.

If I close my eyes and picture that scene, I can still feel the wrestling anguish in my stomach. The natural childhood desire to want to join in and have fun, coupled with its opponent: a gut-clenching fear of doing what I was told was wrong.

I glanced over my shoulder into the house, and down the dark narrow passageway. I could see neither of my parents. The girl stood waiting for my answer whilst I fidgeted with agitation on the step. The fizzy feeling of childhood desire won. Leaping from the step I took the stick and ran towards the others. My fear was forgotten. At last I felt normal. The sun was not the only thing now that brightened my day. I was part of the group I had always longed to play with. Our squeals of excitement rang through the sunny streets. I laughed until my jaw ached. I ran like the wind only this time chased by friends, not enemies or fear. This was freedom, glorious freedom to become the child I was. This was it, this was happiness, and this was heaven where I had never been. I was part of it.

My parents did not appear as everyone else's. One by one all the kids got called in for their tea, and I returned to sit alone on the step.

It was a few minutes of leg swinging before I noticed the first few splashes of tar. Closer inspection revealed that my whole being was speckled. My arms and legs were so covered it was as if a black rash had taken over my limbs. Realisation accompanied with fear overtook me and I started to cry. My mouth was as dry as my face was wet.

I stood up and once more peered into the darkness of the house; no one. Quietly I crept in. I could hear my parents; their heated words travelled from the kitchen along the narrow passageway, confirming that by them, I was forgotten. I placed my hands over my ears as if to hide, thinking if I couldn't hear them they couldn't hear me. I crept into the front room. I took off my shoes to silence my steps. As I walked across the cold floor, my bare feet made a 'tic-tac' noise as they stuck temporarily to the lino. The pounding of my heartbeat racing, the rush of blood resounding in my ears was so loud, I was sure Mum and Dad must be able to hear it. I trembled with fear at the thought that at any moment Dad could appear at the doorway. I looked anxiously around the scantily furnished room for somewhere to hide whilst I tried to clean myself. Squat behind the bulky ancient sofa perhaps? I had done that many a time, hiding with Mum from the debt collectors whilst Dad sat upstairs. No, I needed somewhere safer than that. My eyes fell upon the sideboard. I carefully opened the doors and peered in. There was not much in there, plenty of room for me. I climbed in and pulled the door shut, enveloping myself in the musty smell and safety of the darkness.

Running my hands over my legs I could feel raised bumps of tar all over them; I thought trying to pick them off would be best. Frantically I picked and scratched to remove each speckle, only stopping when tiny trails of sticky blood trickled warmly from my raw wounds. Eventually this action became too painful to carry on.

I do not know how long I was there. Tears welled under my heavy eyelids. I must have silently cried myself to sleep. I was awoken by my mum's voice as she talked to David's mum.

'I dunno where the fuck she is,' Mum was saying. I heard her yell my name over and over again, '*Anna.*' I wondered if she was anxious because she couldn't find me. I am sure this was partly true, but I also knew her underlying worry was Dad's unpredictable temper. Most of the neighbours knew this too.

I screwed up my eyes tightly, thinking somehow this would conceal me even more. I bit my bottom lip trying to stifle a sob rising from my throat, but it escaped anyway, loud enough for Mum to hear.

'Where is she? I can 'ear 'er, but I will be buggered if I can see 'er. Anna!' she yelled, now obviously angry. 'Anna, come on, just stop fucking about and get your arse 'ere now.'

I knew I was beaten and I had to come out. Gingerly I pushed the door of the sideboard open, squinting against the light that invaded my dark sanctuary.

'There you are, come on, get out! What the 'ell are you doing in there anyway? Look at the state of you, and you've pissed yourself.'

Mum grabbed at my arm, dragging me from the cupboard, pulling me to my feet. Her friend came over and peered into the blackness from where I had just emerged.

''Ere, look what she's done to your clean linen.'

Mum loosened her grip from my arm and bent to look.

'Aw, for fuck's sake, as if I don't 'ave enough to do, all that'll 'ave to be washed again.' Her expression changed; a bolt of panic flashed across her face at the realisation. 'Shit, Dick will go mad.'

The thought of Dad being mad made me tremble even more. Once again I felt the warm trickle of urine running away from me. Mum seemed to sense my fear and shoved me hurriedly from the room toward the back yard.

'Get to the bloody toilet, then get back in 'ere and bring the bath with you.'

I returned to the kitchen; Mum methodically filled the tin bath with saucepans of hot water that she had boiled on the stove. David's mum helped her as Dad drank his tea. No one spoke a word.

Dad got up from his chair and came towards me. I knew not to cower if other people were there. This only served to fuel his temper.

'Don't worry, your old dad knows you 'ave to 'ave fun sometimes. Mum will get you clean and the linen will

17

wash.' He ruffled my hair as he spoke, turned, smiled at us all as he pulled a fag from a packet, lit it up, and then went to the front room. 'Oh, Barb, bring me in a mug of tea when you've finished 'er, will you?'

Mum agreed as she carried on scrubbing away at my tar-clad body.

Once I was clean and dressed for bed Mum sent me in to say goodnight to Dad, whilst she saw David's mum out. I hovered at the front room doorway. Mum closed the front door, turned, and ushered me in.

I recall saying goodnight as I kissed Dad's bristle-covered cheek, the spiky hair stabbing my tender face. He leant forward so I could reach, smiling as he did.

'Night, Anna,' he said. He opened his arms, I leant inwards. The unexpected striking blow from his hand landed so hard on the side of my head that it knocked me from my feet, I could not stand. My head reeled as stars flashed before me. 'Get up, get up!' he yelled at me. I struggled to my feet only to have him kick my legs from under me; I hit the floor hard. 'I said get up!' he yelled once more. By now I was sobbing uncontrollably, my mother was crying. He turned to her, pointing his finger 'You shut up,' he shouted. 'And you.' He turned his attention back to me, grabbing my arms, his hands pulling me close; the stench of stale fags filled my nostrils. A wave of nausea swept over me, the weakness that accompanied it buckled me at the knees. 'Stand up straight.' My body automatically jerked to attention at his command. I was close enough to feel the spray of his spit showering over me as he held his twisted angry face close to mine. 'You,' he repeated, lowering his voice. His fit of rage was subsiding, leaving the evil man inside to show himself. 'That will teach you to do as you're told, understand me?' He shook my tiny body with such force the contents of my stomach rose into my mouth.

'Yes, Daddy,' I whispered through the choking sobs that engulfed me. A torrent of verbal abuse followed. Obviously I can't remember exactly what was said but no doubt it went something like this.

'You're a filthy pissy bitch, you deserve what you get; it's your own fault. Now fuck off to bed. I don't want to see you anymore.' I do remember him shoving me into Mum's arms.

Mum's crying had stopped; she stood quietly watching, the usual helpless blank gaze on her face. She ushered me from the room.

'I can't give you any dinner, he'll only moan, and don't wake your brother up with your bawling.' With this she pushed me towards the stairs. 'Get to your bed, go.'

I crawled up the stairs to bed; the spinning in my head would still not allow me to stand. Pulling the one and only blanket over my ears I tried to shut out the world. It rubbed against my already sore legs and arms but I knew I couldn't call for help. I stuffed my fist into my mouth so as not to wake my brother, and cried myself to sleep.

That type of day was pretty typical in our household; most of the time Mum would tiptoe around the outskirts of Dad's temper, trying to keep him happy. Most days she failed and the inevitable arguments would happen. Dad was a control freak with a purely selfish attitude and a violent temper. He was incredibly jealous, possessive and manipulative, turning everything to his own advantage, changing rules to suit himself. His moods were unpredictable and irrational. He was a showman, always fooling anyone who didn't know him well into believing he was the perfect father, husband and gentleman, with his family's best interests at heart. Of course the neighbours knew the truth no matter how hard he tried to cover it, because they heard the screams and shouts. They saw the bruises, the social workers, the endless stream of debt collectors and bailiffs. Their curtains twitched, they spoke about us behind their shiny front doors, and in hushed whispers as they passed us on the streets; but they did not know the full extent of the secrets our house struggled to contain within. They did not hear the whimpers that resounded from our bedroom walls as we lay in pain caused by our bellies being empty for days. There was not enough money for both food and Dad's fags; you can guess which took precedence. They did not hear the threatening whispers that echoed through my head, placed in my brain by the masculine voice beside me, swearing me to secrecy and justifying things I did not understand. When anyone got too nosey or started to ask questions we would up and disappear into the night, just as an apparition; soon those who had voiced their concern would forget us, as if we never existed. By the time we moved into Simpkin Street we had already lived at four different addresses since I was born, and who only knows how many my parents had lived at previous to that.

CHAPTER THREE

It was a little after Christmas 1963. Dad had a job in the local biscuit factory. There was a more regular supply of food on the table, coal for the fire and a much happier atmosphere all round. Even the shouting and beatings Dad still regularly dished out seemed less violent. It was as if I could feel a tangible cloak of contentment wrapping itself protectively around me.

Some nights Mum, Dad and I would leave my brother Carl sleeping peacefully in his cot whilst we went to where Dad worked. Dad would hold my hand, swinging my arm high in the air till giggles burst from my mouth in a fountain of joy. It was always dark but Dad took away my fear by pointing out pictures in the stars, or telling me stories of when he was a boy like the time he blew up frogs by putting straws up their bum and then used them as a football, or when he cried telling the matron at the Barnardo's home where he lived that a boy had beaten him up and stolen his lunch, when really it was the other way round; the boy got punished and Dad got two lunches. Though at the time I saw these stories as funny, I now realise that they were not. The stories just showed that his sadistic behaviour went back a long way.

When we arrived at the biscuit factory we would walk around the back, feeling along the wall, stumbling in the dark. Slipping his hands under my arms he would swing me high over what seemed to be a mountain of empty boxes, dropping me on the other side before wading through the sea of cardboard himself, or kicking it out of the way. All of a sudden he would stop still, a grin would spread across his face and in a loud whisper he would exclaim his apparent surprise at finding a brand new box full of biscuits. 'Anna, Anna, look, pet, look what your dad's found.' I would gasp with amazement. 'That's a bit of magic, that is,' he'd continue just like an excited child. The biscuits were just sitting there under all the empty boxes right outside the factory's rear doors. I was always amazed and shared in his excitement. Obviously I now realise there was no magic in this. He had stolen them earlier during the day, whilst at work, and stashed them outside the doors, ready to return after closing to collect his loot. We would return home with our fantastic find. A few friends and neighbours would come round and Dad would sell the biscuits to them.

I loved these nights; Dad was always happy. His face would shine with pride as he bounced me on his knee. I would shuffle over to make room for Carl to join us. Dad would hug us both, calling me his little lap fitter, and Carl his little man. Long after we had both been put to bed, our bellies full of biscuits and of tea made with watered-down sterilised milk, I would lie and listen with contentment to the chatter and laughter that rose from below. All badness faded away; I could only think how happy I was and how much I loved my daddy for making me so.

The morning would come; Mum would make breakfast for Carl and me. She would take the biscuit crumbs we could not sell and mix them with hot water to make biscuit porridge. We watched her, greedily staring at the concoction emerging into our bowl. Carl would wave his skinny arms and legs about, letting out little squeals of delight as he did so. He had already learnt the meaning of hunger and being deprived. The smooth hot mixture was scraped from my bowl, into my mouth and down into my belly as quickly as I could eat it. There was never enough, but I knew not to ask for more. The broken biscuits that were left were for Dad to dip in his tea; that would keep him happy. A little hunger was a far better thing than facing his wrath, though I knew I would have to, sooner or later. The longer I could stave it off the better. I loved these rare happy times, but even they were no match for how much I loved my brother.

Carl was a little less than a year old. He was an angelic child. He was small for his age, but beautiful; like a small thin version of the heavenly cherubs that we see in famous old paintings. His long, dark, thick lashes framed eyes that sparkled the bluest blue. His hair, thick blond ringlets, one which fell forward onto the creamy skin of his forehead; the others gently kissed the base of his neck. His skin was as pale as the finest porcelain. His doll-like features would break into a smile that lit up the room, and my life, whenever we were together. And I loved him. He would get all the hugs I had to spare. It was him who I protected fiercely with a brave front, standing up to Dad when he lost his temper, taking a hiding for insolence rather than seeing my brother hurt. It was him I lifted from the cot in the middle of the night to hush his whimpers of fear at the rows he could hear. It was him I nursed, kneeling on the bedroom floor, gently rocking back and forth, shushing to sooth the hunger pains in his belly. I was still only three years old, but these things came as second nature from an unknown resource deep within me. Somehow, I just knew what to do.

I must be fair, as I am trying to write this to the best of my ability, as close to the truth as I can remember, but my resource is a child's memories. I never actually saw Dad hit Carl; this is not to say it didn't happen, I just never saw it, though one night it came close, too close.

Carl had been ill; he had even spent some time in hospital. On one particular night, Mum came into our bedroom many times trying to console him. His constant whimpering filled the house with sadness. Nothing she did could settle him. Every time she came in Dad would call her back. I lay in my bed and listened to the argument brewing in the other room.

Snippets of the row remain with me, words, phrases, but some I have to just imagine using the knowledge I have to fill in the blanks.

'Can't you shut the little fucker up? Some of us 'ave work in the morning.' Dad's voice grew louder.

'What do you expect? He's hungry.'

'Well get your tits out then and shut the little bastard up.'

'Don't be so bloody stupid, you know I ain't breastfed since he was born.'

'You're fucking useless, get out the fucking bed you whore, go on, get!' His voice grew louder, booming, enriched with anger. 'I don't fucking want you, you useless piece of shit.' I knew at this point that Dad was probably literally kicking Mum out of the bed.

'Fuck you too,' rallied Mum's angry tearful voice. I heard the thumping of her bare feet slamming down the wooden staircase. Dad reeled a string of obscenities that tumbled after her.

I lifted Carl from his cot. Standing in the middle of the cold dark room, holding him gently, I rocked him in my arms. He sucked on my finger; as I hushed his mournful cries he fell into a fitful sleep. I stood still cradling him gently, but just as firmly as a stray summer cloud holds a welcome shower. I listened to the war that raged outside our bedroom door. I wished it would go away.

'If you won't shut him up I will!' Dad burst into our bedroom. 'What are you staring at?' he shouted. Within seconds he was coming towards me.

I stood rooted to the spot, fear weighing me down, forcing me to stay put. Carl screamed, bringing me to my senses. Suddenly everything clicked. I tightened my arms around him protectively. Dad was close enough for me to feel the heat of his words hit me full force in the face. I had to get away. I backed up, desperately trying to disappear into the shadowy corner of the room. He lunged forward, grabbing my leg, wrenching me away from the wall. My body slammed against the floor. My leg felt as if it were being ripped from its socket, hot searing pain tore through my groin into my stomach as he dragged me back to the middle of the room. I clung desperately to Carl, mostly to protect him but partly to shield me.

'Cover yourself up, you little whore,' he continued, his eyes blazing.

I lay on the floor in just my pants, trembling with fear. Dad let go of me, surveying the room; he prowled around like a trapped animal. He turned to Carl's cot. With one violent kick he put his foot through the wooden bars. All of this happened in what was probably less than a few minutes, but to me it felt like eternity. He turned and left the room to continue pouring out his torrent of rage on Mum.

I sat nursing Carl in my arms for what seemed ages. Not soon enough but eventually, the shouting in the other room stopped; it was replaced by strange grunts, heavy breathing and Mum's childlike giggles. From past experience I knew this meant things had calmed down. I remember asking Mum about the noises; she had said it was Daddy's way of saying sorry to her and telling her he loved her. I told her that I wished Daddy would come and make noises with me. Mum grabbed my arms and shook me; she never did things like that. She told me never to say that again, especially not to Daddy; the special sorry was for her and no one else. She shook me again, shouting at me: *did I understand*? 'Yes,' I replied, but I didn't.

After a while the strange noises gave way to silence, broken only by Dad's occasional snores. Only then did I feel it was safe enough to lay Carl, who was now sleeping, on my bed. I wrapped him in my blanket, changed my sodden pants for clean ones. I wiped the pool of fear-induced urine from the floor with the dirty ones. I didn't want to wake Carl so I curled up on the floor next to my bed and fell into a fitful sleep. In my recurring nightmares, demons with the face of Dad chased me, whilst my mum just looked on.

The next morning I awoke to a silent house. I tiptoed downstairs into the kitchen where my mother stood, holding Carl.

'Mummy?' I questioned; she did not respond. Dad stood still, his face ashen; his hands trembled as he held a match to the fag that hung limply from his mouth. There was a look on his face I had never seen before. I instinctively knew something was very wrong.

The silence was shattered. 'NOOooo.' Mum began to wail. She held Carl in her arms and rocked back and forth. 'NOOooo,' came the cry again. 'Not again not again.' A blood curdling scream erupted from her lips and shook the very ground I stood on. Her voice subsided into muted whimpers that were muffled as she buried her head into Carl's soft ringlets. He was dead.

I was too young to understand. I did not know what death meant, and no one bothered to explain. I waited every day for my brother to come back. Dad wouldn't let me out so I stood at the front room window, lifted the net curtain and gazed the length of the street. I waited hours, no one stopped me, and surprisingly I didn't get told off for being there. I knew that Carl had gone away before, when he went to hospital; but he came back. I remember thinking that this time he was gone a very long while. I wished he would come home. Then one day a car came; it stopped at our house. It must be him; last time he went away he came home by car. The only cars that ever stopped at our house was the telly man's, the one belonging to the man who gave Mum money and she paid back at a bob a week, and the rent man's, and it was none of those. So it must be Carl.

'Carl, Carl.' I almost tore the curtain from its wire as I yanked it over my head. I ran into the hall as fast as I could, just in time to see the arrival of a small pale blue box. It was carried to the front room and put on the sideboard. The man that carried it asked Dad if he wanted to help but he said no, then went into the kitchen and closed the door.

Lots of people came, lots of people cried. At one point Dad even cried, but I don't think Mum did. She sat stony faced. People kissed her and whispered words in her unreceptive ears. I stood for a long time outside the front room door. Why were so many people there? Why were so many people crying? Why was Mummy not talking to me? Had I done something wrong?

Eventually, I went into the room and touched her knee. She looked down at me. A faint flicker of recognition fluttered across her face, then as swift and as quietly as a butterfly, it left. A smile tried to escape from her tightly pursed lips, but it struggled and died before it met her eyes. She raised her hand to touch me, but it fell lifeless into her lap before completing the journey to its so yearned-for destination.

Neighbours stood in the street; the ones that didn't pulled their curtains out of respect. The crowd left our house, and so did the box. I was alone. I knew then, that for some reason, my brother was not coming back.

Though no one had told me, I knew that my Carl was inside that small blue box. Gone for good was the brother I had tried so hard to protect. The brother I had held in my arms willing precious sleep to come his way. The brother I sometimes lay and watched as he contentedly kicked out at the golden sunrays that fell across his cot in the early morning. The brother who had chuckled so much as I took his bare feet to my lips and blew raspberry noises on them.

All that was left on that cool spring morning was a strange silence that attempted to obliterate the hole left in my heart. Though I didn't know it, this was my first experience of true grief.

Many years later I asked Mum about that day, and why no one had explained to me what was going on. She said, '*I can't remember, it was a long time ago, and why bother with all that now?*' I also asked of my other brother Amon. Again, she repeated she had forgotten where he was buried, when he died, and why he died, though once she did say he was born prematurely.

I have since obtained a copy of Carl's and Amon's death certificates. Amon was indeed born premature. He was born and died on Christmas Day 1958. He lived for just ten minutes. The cause of death was indeed premature birth. The post mortem revealed Carl died at home on the first of March 1964. Cause of death was listed as acute otitis media, which in layman's terms is a severe ear infection. Also acute gastritis, which is a sudden inflammation of the stomach lining, caused by a number of different possibilities, such as severe physiological stress, drinking corrosive substances, or a number of other reasons, as well as severe infection. Both of these reasons for death are common everyday illnesses which are not usually fatal, but can be if left untreated. Until the day Dad died, he insisted that when Carl came home, the hospital had said they were letting him come home to die. If that were truly the case, why was his death investigated? Why were such simple illnesses as these left untreated? I have been assured that, unless there were other problems, a child with these illnesses, treated correctly, should have recovered. I can't be sure of what happened, I was only three, but what I can be sure of is that Carl and I were suffering from one other major factor that in my mind no doubt contributed to his death: neglect.

Dad hit me often but rarely hit Mum; deep down I think he was a little scared of her. Though our lives were far different from normality even he knew there was a line he couldn't cross. He would smash or throw anything he could lay his hands on. Verbally he was the most vicious man I have ever known. He gave us all wounds, both physical and mental, that we are still scarred by.

I lived a life of complete submission under the cloud he cast over me with his ways. Life was littered with insecurities and fear, rules changed from one hour to the next. Our house was soulless. Living there was like living in the quiet wake before the onset of a storm; waiting, but never quite knowing when the next clap of thunder would break, or lightning would strike. Occasionally Mum would rise up and argue, but she learnt that it wasn't worth the aftermath, so she dealt with life in her own way. Though he mellowed a little, on the whole this was how Dad was up until the day he died; ironically that was Christmas Day 1994.

CHAPTER FOUR

No one explained to me that Carl wasn't coming back, but somehow I just knew. The weeks that followed his death were the loneliest I had ever known. Night after night I cried myself to sleep. The room that had once rung with my brother's screams now sighed with my quiet whimpers. I had no concept of where he had gone, no idea. No one had ever spoken to me of God or Heaven, but this did not stop me from whispering words into the empty darkness, hoping they were reaching the ears of someone, or something, that would offer me comfort.

Over these weeks a steady stream of people came and went. A mixture of officials poured through our house. They came and sat, rustled their paperwork and left. Some would kneel down to my height, asking me probing questions. They would use their treacle-laden words to sweeten me up, hoping I might slip up and confirm their suspicions that something, although they didn't know what, just wasn't quite right. I would glance over their shoulder just long enough to catch the fleeting look in Dad's eye, the look binding me to silence. The same look that promised unthinkable repercussions if I were to speak of what I heard and saw. The visitor would eventually tire and give up, putting my lack of cooperation down to lack of understanding of the situation.

My parents when questioned would sit in mournful silence. Dad shook his head and stated that he was unable to believe he had lost his only son. Mum held her hands in her lap and sat vacant, silent, an empty vessel, void of all feeling and hope, unable, unwilling to bring to the surface emotions she had locked so deep inside her. Sometimes, I wonder: was this an act? She most certainly had a temper of her own, flying off regularly into a fit of uncontrollable rage. Verbally she could run words with the best of men. Once she was on a roll, the foul poison that flooded from her mouth was vindictive, abusive and damaging to all in its path.

Eventually some normality descended. It was quite a good time. Dad wore his happy face; there was food on the table, coal on the fire and a warm glow throughout. The lack of arguments and violence had unleashed me to run free. Times like these were rare but when they came they would fade all the bad times into shadows of oblivion. I would forget the beatings, the hunger and the verbal abuse that usually clouded my days. Dad became my special daddy; there was none like him. Sometimes when there was just him and me, he would pick me up and sit me on his lap. I would squirm to get away as he tickled me, he would laugh and pull me closer. His eyes would sparkle; shiny beads of saliva gathered at the corners of his laughing mouth. An excited look would cross over his face. He would refuse to put me down, holding me tighter and closer. I think I was a little scared; somewhere I had an instinctive feeling that what he was doing was giving him more pleasure in other ways than just a dad playing with his little girl. His loving attentions were so rare that I did not care and carried on playing until he tired of the game.

I was confused by the sudden change in Dad. Since Carl's death our family had had so much attention. Neighbours were kind and sympathetic and would bring round dinners and leftovers to save Mum cooking. They bought Dad fags and beer. There was understanding for him being off work; many said, 'No one can expect you to go back to work yet after what you've been through.' Dad lapped it up. He strutted around, lorded over the house, and boasted about how he was providing. But if someone gave me a sweet, he would often take it from me, saying, 'Now then, you don't want that, do you? Your good old dad already gets you enough, don't 'e?' I would stand and watch him pop the sweet in his mouth and crunch until there was nothing left, and then he would ruffle my hair and laugh as he walked away. I wanted to cry, but at least he was happy and that was reward enough.

Though I felt sad about Carl, I didn't want to tell anyone. If I did, I knew it would make things go bad again. I didn't want to upset Mum or make Dad angry. I somehow felt guilty and responsible. Could I have protected him more? What if I hadn't held him close on that fateful night? I could have held him behind me and taken the full force of Dad's anger. Would Carl then still be here?

The cold fact was that Carl wasn't there, and things were better for me. I was at last getting the longed-for love and attention that every child deserves. And though I missed him, I found myself wondering if maybe it was for the best. Then in another moment I'd need him so intensely that it was a physical pain, and I would have taken anything, paid any price to get him back.

One day during this happy time, when David's parents were at our house, David and I were sent outside to play in the yard. We must have felt quite courageous because as we tired with our outside games we snuck into the house to spy on the adults. Peeking around the door, I saw Dad lighting David's mum's fag. My mum was sat on David's dad's lap. She had her arms wrapped around his neck as she leant towards him. He whispered secret words in her ear; she threw her head back and laughed. I loved to see her happy, but something just didn't seem right. David giggled loudly.

'Oi, you two.' Mum's bubbly voice reached our secret spying place. David turned and ran down the hallway, with me in hot pursuit.

'Your mum loves my dad,' he taunted me.

'No she doesn't,' I cried in horror. 'Shut up.' My cheeks burned red with embarrassment. Tears of anger ran down my face.

David continued. 'Yes she does, yes she does,' he chanted. David had never teased me like this before. I chased him into the bright sunlight that flooded the back yard. He turned and faced me. 'Yes she does,' he continued, though with uncertainty wavering in his voice. We stood and looked at each other, trying to understand what we had just seen.

'Shut up,' I screamed, and with one swift move I grabbed the lid from the dustbin and hit him squarely over the head with it. 'Now shut up,' I repeated, and I turned and fled indoors before I could see his reaction.

I sat quietly on the bottom stair, my breath coming in short sharp bursts. I was so angry. Mum shouldn't be doing that; why didn't Dad say something? And now I'd hit David. He could be right. Maybe Mum did love his dad? My thoughts bounced around. David's dad was nice, but I wanted my dad. My lip trembled as it tried to hold in the little squeaky sounds that sprung from my stomach to my mouth to accompany the tears that were still arriving unwelcomed at the corners of my eyes. I wanted Mum; I wanted reassurance. Leaving the stairs I went in search of it.

In the front room David was sat on his mum's lap; tracks of disturbed dirt marked his reddened face, a sure sign that I had made him cry. He hadn't told anyone how or why, I was sure of that.

As far as I can recall, David and I did not talk again that day.

The adults had begun to play a game. I leant on the doorway and watched them through the smoky air. The room had the same rancid smell that seeped out from under the doors of the pub on the corner.

I remember walking past the pub and wishing I could see what was behind those big doors that made grown-ups act so funny. Sometimes Mum and Dad would take me there, and sit me outside on the wide stone windowsill. Then they would disappear inside with their friends. Mum would come out with a packet of crisps. Greedily I would open them and rummage to find the little blue bag of salt that was hidden inside, open it and shake it over the crisps. After the blue packet was emptied, I would tear it open and lick any remaining salt from the inside that may have escaped my vigorous shaking. Sometimes I would get a bottle of cream soda or dandelion and burdock, but not often. I would finish my treats and sit and wait. Many nights I would be there until it got dark and beyond. Every time the doors opened I would look up expectantly waiting for my parents to appear, but unless it was chucking out time, it was rarely them.

Occasionally, brawling men spilled through the doors and onto the pavement, scaring me. I would try to squash myself into the dark corner of the deep recessed windowsill and be invisible, at the same time watching with fascination as they tried in vain to stand long enough to swing punches at each other. I could never understand what they were saying, but I knew it was similar to the words that Dad used when he was angry.

When I got cold I would stand on the sill and strain my neck to see above the opaque glass that half covered the window, trying to spot Mum inside. Occasionally she would catch my eye and say something to Dad; in turn he would look at me with a big smile and wave. They would both then turn away, laughing and enjoying themselves, whilst I returned to sit and wait patiently.

I was a quiet child, though not nervous. It seemed even at a young age I found calmness, an inner strength. I was able to understand that for me to protect myself, there were different actions needed for different situations. There were times to be quiet, and try to become virtually invisible, like when Dad was raging, his temper out of control. I learned to be independent, like when I was outside the pub, or hungry, and had to find a way of getting food. There were also times to keep my words away from my lips, imprisoning them inside me; these were perhaps the hardest of all. Some of the grown-ups that visited would ask me things like 'Does Daddy cuddle you lots?' or 'Does Daddy smack you when you are naughty?' One particular lady I remember had a lovely soft cardigan and smelt of lily of the valley perfume; her smile was warm and loving. I longed to go home with her. What I wanted to do was ask her, why did my daddy do this? Why was I so hungry? Why could I not play like the other kids? Were all dads like this? But Dad always made sure when anyone pried I was hushed. He would often speak for me, putting words like *Oh, she don't understand, she don't know what she's talking about* in place of my silence. Sometimes he would put his hand protectively over my shoulder or pull me onto his lap; his fingers dug into my flesh, unable to be seen by the questioning party, but enough for me to know it was one of those times to stay silent.

There were certain special times when I didn't have to, when I could open my heart and tell all. This was when Big Nan visited.

Big Nan was my mum's mum. She lived in London and rarely did she come to stay. Now that Carl had gone, she was the only person that I truly trusted. I loved her visits. When she was there my world took on a whole new meaning. Dad said she spoilt me. In all honesty she didn't; she treated me like the small child that I was.

On the day she was coming I would sit on the step. It wouldn't matter how long I sat there, all day if I had to; I was used to that anyway. It was worth it for that first glimpse of my Big Nan. From where I sat I could see down to the end of our street and up towards Bluebell Hill. Somewhere up the hill was the train station; I can't remember how far away it was. I would strain my eyes, some days through the dazzling summer sun and others through the rain that had collected in small droplets that clung to my eyelashes, and wait.

Nothing could have replaced the feeling that overcame me within the first few seconds of seeing her. Her tall, slim, distinguished figure would appear over the horizon. She walked briskly towards me, her stride determined and strong, almost a march. Her large shiny handbag would swing from her arm, a pendulum movement in perfect time with her steps. I would always know it was she. As she grew nearer, I would stand up and jump up and down waving both my arms in the air, never shouting or calling her, as I didn't want Mum and Dad to know she had arrived. If they did they would spoil my first few moments with her. As soon as she saw me she would raise her hand, her steps would quicken and that was my signal. With unbridled love I would leave the step and run, run as fast as my legs would carry me. My heart pounding so hard in my chest I thought it would escape and bounce up the road by itself just to be with her! When I was a safe distance from home and Big Nan was within my reach I would call her, call as loud as I could. Tears would envelop us both as we clashed in unison, holding each other as if we would never let go. Big Nan would always kneel down to my height. Her eyes shone brighter than the nearest star. No doubt the sparkle enhanced by her captured tears.

'Hello my old flower.' She would always call me this.

'Hello my old flower too,' I would always reply.

Eventually she would slip her warm soft hand into mine and we would start the descent to home together.

Her arrival was always the same. On the first day Dad would be sickly nice. Mum would busy herself trying to

36

cook a half-decent meal with the meagre supplies she had in the cupboard. I would sit snuggled as close to Big Nan as I could. Her warmth radiated not only from the protective arm she kept wrapped around me, but also from her heart.

The first night she arrived Dad always saw as an opportunity to go out. He would say, 'Do you mind, Nell, if I take Barb out? Only we so rarely go out together, we don't like leaving Anna with anyone.' He would smile at her, trying to portray that perfect father image that he saved for anyone but me. He was telling the truth, he didn't like leaving me with anyone; because, by this stage, it was rare I would be allowed to go with them, usually I was put to bed and left on my own.

'You go on. We'll be all right here, won't we, my old flower?'

Eagerly I would agree, longing for the peace that descended after the closing of the door when they left.

Once they were gone, she and I would curl up on the settee. She would fish in her cardigan pocket and pull out two toffees or mint humbugs. She would slowly unwrap them, watching me from the corner of her eye as she did so. I tried not to look longingly at the sweets. Though I knew she would never hurt me I was virtually brainwashed into the controlled behaviour that was forced upon my everyday existence and found it very difficult to act differently with anyone, even someone I loved and trusted as much as her.

'So tell your old nan what's been going on, then.'

I recall hanging my head in shame, fearful of what to say. Her soft finger would always gently lift my chin before popping the delicious sweet in my mouth. Her protective loving arm wrapped back around my shoulders and pulled me close. She smelt the same as the lady visitor I had wanted to go home with. We sat quietly, the silence only broken by the crackle of the fire she had made, and the sucking of the sweets we shared.

Big Nan knew there were problems. She knew exactly what Dad was like, and what Mum had become. She would never press me to talk, or worry me into telling her things, but that one question whilst sharing the intimate moment by the fire was usually all the encouragement I needed to tell her all my worries. I would snuggle closely into her side; my head nestled on her lap. As I spoke she would stroke my hair. Sometimes she was so quiet I thought she must be asleep, but then I would feel her body shake with a little sob, or a wet tear plop on to the top of my head. She never broke my confidence, though in the following days of her visit, I would lie in bed and listen to the heated exchange of words between her and my parents. I knew that whilst she was there, Dad would not dare hit me. Though a bully, he was also a coward. Big Nan was my saviour and I was then and always will be eternally grateful.

As an adult, I have had a great deal of trouble accepting that my childhood was abusive. Even though logically I know that what happened to me was severe mental, physical and, at times, sexual abuse, it still makes it no easier to acknowledge. One of the clever things about abusers is their ability to make the victim think that in some way they bring the abuse upon themselves. Even though I know this isn't the case, somewhere that conviction still lingers. I read articles and books of others that have been abused, some much worse than me. I have had to learn to turn a deaf ear to the voice inside me that whispers how lucky I was not to go through what they went through, and that perhaps what happened to me wasn't abuse at all, but that I did truly deserve it. Closing my ears to the inner voices that still haunt my darkest quiet moments has enabled me to write this and recover to be the person I am now.

CHAPTER FIVE

All of the time I lived with my parents was spent moving from one place to another. I left home at the age of 17; we had lived in no less than 25 different places. This calculation is done from memory and without including the times we were homeless or sleeping on friends and relatives' floors or sofas.

By the time we got to Simpkin Street I had already lived in several other homes, all of them in Nottingham.

After Carl died a few of the neighbours around us seemed to take more notice of me. One of these, a man whose name escapes me, I remember seeing for the first time in the shop on the corner of our road.

I had been hanging round Mum desperate for something to eat. I must have been exceptionally hungry because it was not like me to complain; I was too scared of the repercussions. Anyway, Dad came into the kitchen where we were and bent down towards me.

'Here, have this.' He pushed a crisp paper note into my hand. 'Go to the shop and get yerself summat.'

I held up the paper money he had given me; on it was printed 'one pound'.

'Aw, Dick, it isn't fair to give 'er that.'

Dad's eyes left my bemused face and looked at Mum.

'She wants it, don't you?' he questioned, his eyes returning to mine. I nodded eagerly. 'Off with you then, go on, go spend it.' He smiled as he pushed me towards the door.

I walked up the hall and out of the house, pulling the door shut behind me. I stood for a moment on the step, unable to believe my luck, looking once again at what Dad had given me. I had no idea of how much a pound was or what it could buy, but what I did know was it could put an end to the groaning pain that thundered around my tummy.

A squeal of delight escaped my smiling lips as I leapt from the step, jumped off the kerb and ran across the road to the shop on the corner. If there had been more traffic about I would surely have been flattened, but as it was a car was a rare and exciting appearance in our street. If one did appear and it stopped, all the children, me included, would gather round and stare in the windows. The driver and passengers would stand little chance of getting out without being mobbed by an army of questions being fired rapidly from the mouths of innocent inquisitive children. ''Ow fast does it go, mister?' 'Is it yours?' 'Cor, are you rich?' were just a few. Most of the cars that stopped in our street were owned by tallymen, social workers, rent collectors or bailiffs.

I arrived at the shop. As I pushed open the door a loud ringing sound echoed above my head, startling me. The occupants inside turned to see who had come in.

'Hello, you're the young lass from across the road, aren't you?' The shopkeeper who was asking smiled welcomingly. I nodded and smiled back. I had been in the shop before with Mum but never alone. Usually we just went in, did our business and came out again, often empty-handed. There was a big note above the counter that read 'NO CREDIT'; I used to watch the man point it out and read it to Mum.

Today was different; I could walk around and look at all before me. Fresh crusty loaves sat on the counter sending tempting smells to tickle my nose. Next to them underneath a large glass dome was a mound of butter. I stood and watched fascinated as the shopkeeper removed the lid and

40

scooped a lump onto a slab of marble; with two grooved paddles he splattered and patted the butter until it roughly resembled the shape of Dad's fag packet. He then nimbly lifted it with one of the paddles and placed it onto a sheet of greaseproof paper. He swiftly wrapped it up into a perfect bundle and passed it to the man standing in front of him.

In front of the counter was a bench on which sat all manner of fruit and vegetables. Nowhere near the likes of the selection of today but nonetheless to my hungry eyes a treasure chest of goodies.

Behind the counter were rows of shelves; one row contained shiny glass jars. Sweets of all kinds lived in these. Velvet toffees, fruit bonbons, sweet peanuts, gobstoppers as big as your eye, pear drops, humbugs, cough candies. All called me with their enticing voices. On another shelf sat the half-penny sweets, Black Jacks, Fruit Salads, liquorice laces and spearmint chews. These were followed by fat glass jars of sherbet, pink, yellow and orange, sure to turn your fingers and tongue the same colour as it when you ate it. The very last jar on the shelf made me gasp with delight, traffic light lollies, red and rosy; some gave a little glimpse of the colour that was hidden below the shiny surface, green, yellow. My mouth watered at just seeing them. The man behind the counter saw me looking.

'One of these, lass?' he asked as he took the jar from its place. I watched my distorted image reflecting in the thick glass jar he held before me, my head nodding so vigorously it's a wonder that it didn't actually come loose!

'A penny,' he requested as I dutifully passed over the now pretty creased pound note, at the same time popping the lolly into my eager mouth.

My taste buds burst into life, my jaw physically ached with the pleasure of the sweet sour taste that rushed over my tongue and washed round my mouth. My eyes closed, as I sucked loudly, so loudly that I did not hear the shopkeeper talking to me. In fact the first acknowledgement I gave the outside world was a yelp when the lolly was cruelly ripped from my mouth.

'You little toe rag; you're just like your dad. Go on, be off with yer.'

I had no idea what I had done. He grabbed my arm and started marching me to the door. Tears of anger sprung to my wide eyes. I struggled furiously, kicking and screaming as I tried to break free from his grasp and his fingers dug into the tender flesh of my arms. I don't think I noticed the pain he was causing me, it was trivial compared to what I was used to; but what on earth had I done wrong?

'Steady,' a man's voice said. 'She's only a wee 'un.' It was the butter man.

'Don't you let her fool you; she is just like the rest of 'em, little thief.' He shook me a little as he spoke, just to emphasise his words. I had no idea what was going on. My cheeks burned hot with embarrassment; he clearly thought I had done something. That upset me but not half as much as the biting comment that beat my ears, whipping straight to my heart; I was not like my dad, I didn't want to be like my dad.

'Here, I'll pay for the lolly.' The man held out a threepenny bit. Momentarily the shopkeeper loosened his grip; it was just long enough for me to shake myself free and bolt for the door. Flinging it open I ran; his angry voice chased me. I ran so fast that by the time I reached the safety of my front step I felt my lungs would burst. Every breath sent a torrent of fire through my body; even the flood of my tears wouldn't put out the fire of embarrassment that burnt in my cheeks. I must have been gasping so noisily that Mum heard me because she threw open the door and dragged me inside.

'Look at the state of her; funny, is it?' She paraded my breathless body in front of Dad. 'You total bastard. It was cruel giving her Monopoly money. You might have known the shit in the shop would give her a thick ear.'

Mum threw her voice full force at Dad. She was sticking up for me. I was so pleased, it stemmed my tears immediately. The only thing was I still didn't understand what I had done wrong. Dad smiled, but as Mum raved on, his smiling lips took on a harder line, and his eyes sent hot poker looks that split the air between us.

'Fuck off.' That was all he said.

Mum and I did; she took me out for a walk. As we walked she explained that the money was only pretend and I couldn't buy anything with it. She said Dad had done it for a joke. But I think she knew just as well as I did that it was a joke that only he saw the funny side of, because it was at someone else's expense.

So that was my first meeting with the man from up the street. Over the next few weeks I saw him regularly; he would be walking down the road or in the shop or sometimes just standing around. Occasionally he would call me over to him and give me a sweet or an apple. Once he asked me to his house; I went skipping merrily beside him. He promised me a drink of orange when we got there. I had never had orange. All we ever drank in our house was water or weak tea made with diluted sterilised milk.

I had only been in the man's house a few minutes when my parents banged on the door. Dad started shouting, calling the man rude names that I didn't understand. 'Paedophile' was not a common word then and even if it were he would have been too ignorant to use it, but I am sure the words he used meant exactly that.

Dad dragged me from the house, tugging me so hard that my feet hardly touched the ground.

I remember the incident with clarity; some of the words Dad used stuck in my brain, furrowing the first grooves for the seeds of insecurity and self-hate to flourish in as my life trundled on.

'Whore, little slut, gonna suck his cock were you for a sweetie?' I didn't even know what a cock was. He was walking so fast I had no chance of keeping up.

'Whore.' He slapped me around the back of the head. 'Whore.' He repeated his action again. Mum hurried behind, desperate to catch up.

'Dick, Dick, stop it, Dick, wait.' She was sobbing.

'She's a whore in there with him. Don't tell me she is innocent. She's a whore, a prick tease.'

This went on all the way to our front door. Dad threw me into the house. One well-aimed kick sent me skidding along the hall floor. I scrambled, my feet desperately trying to grip on the shiny lino surface. Succeeding, I ran for my life. I did not stop running until I was up the stairs and in my room. I stood there, back against the door, placing my hands over my ears. I tried to block out the screaming voices that battled below. I listened to my own short sharp breaths, in, out, in, out. My heart beat hard enough to bounce my dress clear from my chest. My knees buckled and I sat in a crumpled heap on the floor. Once again I had done wrong; but what had I done? I had caused another argument. No matter how hard I tried I couldn't work out why I just couldn't be good.

I remember many things from this time in my life, some bad and some not so bad. There were most certainly times I would say were good times, when Dad was so funny he made us laugh hard enough for it to hurt; he would pull faces and chase me round the house. Just for that short time he loved us unconditionally, as it should be. Those good memories are marked as clear in my mind as the bad ones. The days I don't remember are the ones that rolled by; these consisted of regular slaps round the back of my head or kicks up my arse. Times of tummy rumbles and hunger, not the excessive hunger I spoke of earlier but just general hunger when I had missed a meal or two. What I call these normal days also consisted of waiting on Dad, serving him tea, getting his fags and trying to do as I was told. He often asked me to tickle his feet with my fingers or a pencil. He said it was his favourite game. I would sit on the floor, my back against the chair where he sat, and hold his foot in my lap. Dad would say *softer* or *harder, don't look at me, watch what you're doing*. I would always try to do it the best I could because sometimes he would give me a penny.

Occasionally Dad would let me and Mum go to the shops alone. Mum never seemed very keen. I thought she didn't want to be with me. Looking back now I realise her lack of enthusiasm had nothing to do with that at all, it was probably more the pressure of his demands, expecting us to nick whatever we could to fulfil the list that he had given us before we left. What we couldn't nick, we were sent out to beg or borrow from the neighbours.

Sometimes Dad would come into town with us, insisting I be in my pushchair even though I was quite capable of walking. He would encourage me to smile at strangers. They would often comment on what a lovely child I was and what a beautiful smile I had. Often they would give me a penny or more which Dad would rapidly take as soon as they turned their back, and push into the depths of his own pocket, never to be seen by me again.

Then came the day that changed everything.

A stiff breeze took my short dark curls and whipped them across my face as I sat on the step of Simpkin Street. I knew something was going on but I didn't know what. I was told not just to sit on the step but to go play with the other kids on the bombsite at the bottom of the hill. I didn't need telling twice. I was gone. I must have played for hours. We chucked stones at cans, at boys and then in anger at each other; we soon made it up though. We played a game called 'It', running around with boundless joyful energy. One of the girls even let me wobble with her much prized hula hoop. As usual everyone else got called in for their tea until eventually I was the only one left. I sauntered up to my house, no doubt kicking and scuffing the toes of my already well-worn shoes. I recall being angry. Why did everyone else get dinner when I didn't?

I reached home just as dusk was falling. Something felt different; I didn't know what. I pushed the front door but it didn't move. Using both hands I shoved it even harder but still nothing. I hammered my fist against the hard wood surface and put my ear to the door to listen for sounds within. All I could hear was my own breath. I sat on the step to wait.

Dusk soon turned into darkness, I waited patiently. All I had on was my day clothes, little more than a thin cotton dress. Though it was not winter I was cold so I curled up on the doorstep. It must have got late because my eyes were heavy and soon I fell asleep.

The next thing I knew strong arms were lifting me. Too young, too tired and too cold to register I snuggled into this warm human being. I suppose I thought it was Mum or Dad, but it wasn't.

The next morning I woke in a strange room. The bed I was in was covered in a thick warm blanket. The sun shone through the gap in the curtains. I could hear someone moving around downstairs. I didn't know whether to be scared or not. Whoever this was had obviously been nice to me. I remember thinking perhaps I was dead like Carl and this place was heaven. Big Nan had told me all about Heaven and told me that Carl was living with Jesus who looked after him. According to her Carl had all the toys and food he could ever want. Sometimes, when I was really hungry or I had made Dad really cross I wished I could be dead too.

I was still fully dressed. I jumped from the bed and pushed my feet into my shoes which had sat all night to attention on the floor and waited. Slowly I crept to the top of the stairs. The house was the same layout as ours but apart from that the inside was a million miles away. For a start there was a rug on the bedroom floor; the stairs had carpet too, not all over, just a strip down the middle. It was held to the stairs with shiny brass rods. I trod carefully as I crept down them. I was curious and scared at the same time but neither of these senses won over the temptation of the delicious aroma that drifted to my nostrils and beckoned me to find its source.

'There you are. I was just gonna wake you. You've been sleeping for ages, you 'ave, me girl.' It was the lady next door. 'Come on, sit, eat.' In front of me she placed the biggest bowl of porridge I had ever seen; over it she spooned syrup. 'Well go on then, eat up, it don't bite.' Greedily I shovelled the steaming concoction into my mouth.

'You like that then?' I nodded, too busy eating to answer properly. 'Good.' She smiled and turned away, mumbling quietly but not quietly enough; I heard her say, 'Probably the first good meal the child's ever 'ad in 'er.'

I don't actually remember returning home or what reason Mum and Dad gave for not being there. Years later I asked; according to Mum they went away for a few days and he thought she had arranged a sitter and she thought he had. That's one version; the other she has said is that she was rushed into hospital to have a baby so she could not let anyone know where she was. I think the first is more probable because I don't remember any new baby; also Dad had never been and never went to a hospital with Mum for as long as he was alive, not through births, illness or even visiting, so why would he have gone then? Anyway, why overnight? I always laugh at the fact that he was scared of hospitals yet always insisted he was ill. It's a bit of a funny phobia for a hypochondriac, isn't it?

Shortly after that incident it happened, as sudden and unexpected as a clap of thunder on a sunny day; overnight my life seemed to change. The first I knew of it was when I was woken in the early hours.

'Anna, Anna, come on, you got to get up.' Mum shook me gently. 'We are going on a train to see Big Nan.' I rubbed my eyes sleepily. The big curtains were open so I could see a vast expanse of inky blackness outside my window. 'Come on, quick, hurry, get dressed.' She ushered me into my clothes. 'Keep quiet; we don't want to wake the craggy bag next door.' I don't know why Mum called her that; she was always nice to me, especially since I had slept at her house.

We all went out into the night. Dad carried a big bag; so did Mum. I carried Andy Pandy, my black and white panda bear. I had had him for so long that I couldn't remember not having him. Dad said I had to leave him at the house but I started to cry. I think he was worried about the noise I was making so eventually he gave in and let me take him, but he was all I was allowed to take; all my other possessions, what few there were, had to stay.

The train we caught was called the milk train. It was cheaper to travel that way.

As morning broke we pulled into Woolwich Arsenal Station. We stepped onto the deserted platform. I remember the fear I felt as the train pulled away. To me that was the last connection I had with the life that I had been forced to leave behind. The unknown lay ahead. As it turned out I am glad I didn't know what was to come.

We went to stay at Big Nan's. She had a flat in a big house in Woolwich, south-east London. When we arrived she tucked me into her enormous bed. The bed was covered with a plum-coloured silk bedspread that felt cool and soft against my skin. Though I trusted her, when she turned and left the room fear of being in a strange place enveloped me. I lay and listened to the voices coming from the other room. Placing my hand down my pants and wiggling my fingers gave me a comforting feeling. I knew someone had shown me how to do this at some time but I didn't and still don't remember who. The door opened; it was Big Nan checking to see if I was asleep. I didn't stop what I was doing because I didn't know it was supposedly wrong to do. All I knew was someone had done this to me before and it felt nice. So when she came across the room and slapped my hand hard I was devastated. Big Nan had never slapped me. I lay there stunned.

'Don't dare do that, you dirty girl.' What? What had I done? My bottom lip trembled as I tried to hold back the tears forced forward by the feeling of shock and humiliation.

Big Nan stormed from the room. I could hear her shouting at Dad and he was shouting back. After what seemed eternity there was the slam of a door and then silence. I crept to the bedroom door and opened it just enough so I could peek out. Was I alone? I had been alone before. No, there I saw Big Nan. She was holding her head in her hands. Her whole body trembled. A sixth sense must have told her that I was there because she turned and looked at me. Her smile through her veil of tears was all I needed to see. I ran to her arms. 'Don't be crying, my ol' flower, it's all right, I won't do it again.' All I knew was that my innocent actions had made her cry, but that wasn't it; it was who or what had taught me those things that made her so sad.

I don't know how long we stayed at Big Nan's. After a while we moved into a home of our own. The flat we moved into took up the whole middle floor of a detached Victorian house on Wrottesley Road in Plumstead. Around the same time we moved in a new baby arrived. His name was Andrew.

When Mum brought Andrew home he was small. I knew he was born early because Big Nan had told me, but nothing prepared me for the tiny delicate being that came home with Mum. He was placed on my lap, a small warm bundle sleeping. He made gentle snuffling noises as he nestled deeper against my warmth.

'Enough now, put 'im down, we don't want 'im to get spoilt, do we?' Dad had spoken. Mum lifted Andrew from my arms but just as she did he opened his eyes. I was faced with the same sparkling eyes that Carl had fixed me with when I held him. Andrew's gaze held mine; a secret message of trust travelled between us, a fierce pledge of comradeship. I knew that from that moment he was mine to protect and I his to love and rely on. I would not let him die.

I don't have a lot of bad memories from our time at Wrottesley Road, though in the end it proved to be one of the worst times of my life.

The house was filled with two other families as well as us. The family that lived on the top floor consisted of three boys and their parents. Downstairs lived a woman and her son. Though she was married her husband worked away a lot so she was often on her own for weeks at a time.

All in all, the whole household and the surrounding neighbours got on well. I have memories of a big garden where we all played. Someone, maybe even I, had a paddling pool. I still have a photo of all the kids from the house sitting in it squashed side by side, trying to cool ourselves on a hot sunny day. We wore an array of swimsuits and baggy knickers. The one thing we all had in common was that we all looked incredibly happy.

As Andrew grew he developed a habit of rocking on his chair, at times so hard he would bang his head on the wall behind him. This habit angered Dad. Andrew was too young to realise that he was causing such anger so carried on regardless. Every time I could I used to rush to stop him doing it, distracting him by pulling faces or singing to him. Dad used to sing to him too, a song that went something like... *'They're coming to take you away, ha ha.'* And also *'Ha ha ha, hee hee hee, I'm a lucky fella and you can't catch me.'* Andrew laughed, over and over; he loved everyone unconditionally. Probably a lot like me, he craved his love to be returned and would forgive injustice and abuse at the drop of a hat for a cuddle or a bit of attention. This didn't change the irrational unpredictable temper that Dad rained upon us. Many days I stood and took a slap, a kick or even a punch to protect Andrew. There was no way I was going to let any thing happen that might harm him. In my mind I hadn't protected Carl properly, I had failed him and he had gone and died.

One day Andrew's head banging was particularly annoying Dad. Even though I was only six, I sensed danger creeping its ugly way forward. Nothing I did helped. Eventually Dad's temper broke. The sudden slap knocked Andrew clean off his chair. I dived forward to try to come between them, hoping, as on many occasions before, I could take the brunt of Dad's anger to protect my brother. I took a hiding but only for my actions; at least Andrew only got one hit.

Days later Andrew was admitted to hospital. He was in some time though I can't remember how long. When he came home he only had one eye. I have since learnt that when he got to hospital he had a fractured skull and a brain tumour. To remove the tumour they had to remove his right eye.

When Andrew came home we became inseparable. After a while Mum, Andrew and I went on a train to the London Eye Hospital to choose him a new eye. I clearly recall being in a room, Mum with Andrew on her lap and me sitting on a chair next to them. The man we were seeing left the room and returned with a tray containing row after row of glass eyes. Each one was carefully lifted and placed next to Andrew's good eye to try to get the best colour match possible. I was terrified, sitting rigid, looking at all those eyes. I don't know how long we were there but I know when we left Andrew had two eyes again.

Dad and Mum took to going out more; nothing had changed. Andrew and I spent many hours together. He, though less than two years old, had learnt to torment me. He would press his finger on the bottom of the socket of his false eye and pop it from its place into the palm of his hand; he would then chase me with it. Though it no longer frightened me, I let him think it did. I would scream with mock fear just to see his delighted face burst into an array of smiles followed by our infectious giggles flooding the room. His brightness was second only to looking directly at the sun on a hot summer's afternoon, blindingly wonderful.

Recently I got Mum to talk; it is so rare she does this that I listen attentively, taking in every detail. She now states that Andrew was the baby born on the night I was left alone. I recently obtained his birth certificate which indeed confirms he was in fact born in Nottingham. I don't remember him coming home or travelling to London with us but that does not mean he didn't. Maybe the sheer grief of losing Carl did not allow my acknowledgement of Andrew for some time and the memory I have of him coming home was maybe indeed to Nottingham. Truthfully I do not know whether he came straight home after birth or not. No relative that I can ask remembers. It seems the truth is lost in the past and will remain that way.

CHAPTER SIX

Autumn 1966, the headlines of the morning paper read how tragedy had struck two families in Wrottesley Road, south-east London. The house in which they lived had caught fire; a young boy and a woman had died in the blaze.

I had no recollection of the fire until the last few years. I only knew what I had been told. The mind is a wonderful piece of machinery that sometimes shuts the door on certain areas in order to provide security and protection for the rest of its necessary actions. That is what mine did. For years I had no memories of any of the events either immediately pre or post the fire. I knew that parts of my adult life were in complete turmoil because of some of my unexplainable actions and feelings, but that was all. Eventually, in my forties, and with support from my husband and wonderful GP, I sought help. Now I can recall parts of the fateful day that changed my life so much for the worse.

The day of the fire was much the same as any other; in fact I don't really remember it at all. Apparently Mum and Dad had gone to have a drink with the woman downstairs. Dad has since told me it was her anniversary and she was fed up as her husband was working away so they went down to cheer her up.

Mum tucked us up to sleep in the bedroom we all shared. I now remember snuggling down in my bed which was situated one side of the big Victorian bedroom and looking across at Andrew sleeping peacefully in his cot on the other. A chink of soft creamy light splayed from the streetlight outside and crept through the gap left in the curtains, casting eerie shadows across the vast bay window and into the room. Even at this young age I was not frightened to be alone; in fact in some ways I preferred it. All I had to do was look after me and Andrew. There was no looking over my shoulder, no walking on tiptoe, no worrying whether I would say the right thing or even whether to say anything at all lest undeserved repercussions come either of our ways.

Voices echoed from the dark street below as people passed by. They were reassuring; someone somewhere was still awake, and though I would never dare, my subconscious knew that if needed I could always call for help. I knew even though I was only six I was completely responsible for looking after Andrew that night and no matter how tired I was I would not let my heavy eyelids close until I knew he was OK.

The next memory I have is of sitting on the floor under the big bay window. I was holding Andrew in my arms. He was coughing uncontrollably. I nuzzled my face into his downy blonde hair, stroking his forehead as I murmured soft words to try to reassure him. Instinct told me something was seriously wrong. The light that flowed in from the window had disappeared. I tried in vain in the denseness to reach for the curtains. I wanted to pull them open and shout for help. I knew Andrew would be scared but I just couldn't hold him and do it.

'I have to put you down, Andrew; I need to call Mummy from the window.' At least he had stopped coughing. I lay his limp body on the floor beside me. I was relieved my rocking and hugging had sent him to sleep. I struggled to stand, the air was so thick. My eyes were stinging. I could not breathe. A burning sensation rushed over my gasping lips down my throat and into my lungs. I remember no more.

I lay still and let the unusual sounds flood over me. The muzzy awareness of strange surroundings filtered through to my sleepy brain: dull voices, the chinking of china, a cough. Strange smells filled my nostrils; rancid, antiseptic smells that reminded me of the cream Big Nan put on my skinned knees whenever I fell. Mum, I wanted my mummy. I tried to call for her but the searing pain that shot through me paralysed my words before they could form on my tongue. I knew I wanted to wake up, I had to wake up but somehow I just didn't. I don't know how long I lay there in this state. Trapped in a body that would not respond to what my mind was telling it. Not knowing where I was but aware of everything around me, no one knowing I was awake.

Eventually someone was there next to me, talking, I could hear their words.

'Poor little mite, don't know how she survived. It's a miracle, that's what it is, though the doctor says she may never see again. Look at the state of her little face. Her parents weren't even in, you know; ought to be shot they should, put away for life.'

The cool water which was being dabbed on my face felt good. For a second I let the tenseness flood from my body. I must have let out a sigh because the person beside me called my name.

'Mummy?'

I heard the sharp intake of breath from one of the voices.

'Hello, dear; no, I'm not Mummy, I'm a nurse, you're in hospital.' She held my hand as she spoke, stroking her fingers across mine.

'I'll go and get the doctor,' another voice said.

The days that followed were literally blind confusion, as I lay there and tried to piece together what had happened. I had no sight; I was completely blind. I also had intense pain with every breath that I took. The smoke damage to my eyes was so bad the doctors were unsure if I would ever get my full vision back. The pain I was in was caused not only by

55

the smoke inhalation, but also by the heat. My lungs, throat and nose were literally scorched. When the fireman rescued me I had stopped breathing; I took so long to resuscitate that the medical team didn't hold out much hope, but they didn't know what a fighter I was. I had fought all my life to survive; it was an instinctive action.

Over the next few weeks I regained my sight, but I had to have drops in for ages. I screamed when this was done, they stung me just as much as the smoke had, but the nurses convinced me they would make me better and slowly but surely they did.

Eventually I returned home to a sparsely furnished flat on the top floor of a house overlooking Plumstead Common. Everything was different. There was even less furniture than usual. I had even less clothes, just what I stood up in and one other dress. I wanted Andy Pandy desperately but he was gone. I was still very frail and I think even Dad knew he had to be careful.

Days, maybe even weeks went by. I slept a lot. My mental state was in tatters. I was terrified of the dark and had to have lights on wherever I went, in every room before I would go in, even in the daytime. I couldn't stand the curtains being closed, and even though the cold rushed in I had to have the windows slightly open in every room. I would not leave Mum's side, clinging to her and screaming. She couldn't leave me even to go to the toilet.

A while later, I don't know how long, I was sat at the kitchen table. Mum sat one side and I was on Dad's knee on the other.

'Where's Andrew?' I asked. Silence met me. Mum looked down at her hands where they rested on her knees. Dad shifted slightly on the chair.

'He's dead, isn't he? He's not coming home, is he?' This was a statement more than a question. I knew, I just knew.

Surprisingly enough it was Dad that answered me.

'No, no, he's not coming home, he's gone. But we're lucky, though; it could have been Mum. The lady who lived in the top flat died and she left her three boys, so we're lucky, aren't we?'

I didn't feel lucky. Of course I didn't want Mum to be dead but I didn't want Andrew to be dead either. In fact I didn't want anyone to be dead. I didn't feel lucky, I felt like I wanted to cry. A lone tear plopped on the Formica table in front of me.

'OK.' Mum's voice cut through my impending grief. 'Enough, it will be Christmas soon. What do you want for Christmas?'

She was asking me what I wanted for Christmas. Waves of anger crashed against the shores of my grief, drowning my sorrow and replacing it with a scrubland of anger, deformed and scarred, littered with the washed-up rubbish and debris from the years before. It all came at once. I wanted to scream at her, *I want my brother back! I want you to never leave me! I want to stop being scared!* But I kept silent until I knew I could control what I was about to say. Slowly I raised my fallen chin from where it sat sunken into my chest. My gaze met hers. Steadily I captured and held the attention of her faded blue eyes, imprisoning her with my gaze.

'I want a fire engine,' I replied. Emphasising the words slowly and clearly I repeated what I had said. 'I want a big red fire engine.' With that I jumped from Dad's knee and left the two of them sitting there.

Those minutes set me free from the prison I was locked in. I was still terrified of the dark, still scared of what might be, but I knew Mum was not the one to protect me, and certainly nor was Dad. No, I had to do that myself. I had to rely on just me, to trust no one.

I closed the door to my room. For once Dad let me be. At first I sat on the edge of the bed in silence. Slowly the tears came. One by one they followed each other down the myriad of tracks which traced their path down my face. My body started to convulse as heaving sobs from deep within racked my body. Uncontrollably I cried out as I fell to the floor. I don't know how long I lay there, till my grief was spent, till there were no more tears, no more breaths of sorrow and sadness. Until I accepted that I had let another brother die.

I found out years later the investigation into the fire proved that it had started in two places in the lounge. One, the curtains seemed to have caught fire, but at the same time the fire had also started down the inside of the sofa between the cushions. It was never established as to how.

Dad said that we had a faulty telly that often overheated. He had complained to the people we rented it from but they had said there was nothing wrong with it. He also said on the night of the fire he and Mum knew that the sound of the telly would be comforting to us so he had left it on but taken the back off to help it keep cool. The telly was under the window and therefore he also opened the window to cool it down. Dad's version is that the curtains blew onto the hot valves in the back of the telly and caught fire; the draught from the window fanned the fire into a blaze. This is possible but doesn't explain the fire starting down the side of the sofa. Dad's version of that was that the woman next door was a chain smoker; she had been round before Mum and Dad went out and must have dropped her fag. It must have smouldered for a while and then eventually burst into flames at the same time as the curtains.

The local paper showed a picture of our cooker. The heat in the flat was so great that it had melted; the metal sides buckled and bowed, making it virtually unrecognisable. My brother was probably dead when I laid him on the floor to try to get help. His death certificate states asphyxiation from smoke inhalation.

The lady in the flat above tried to jump from the roof but broke her neck when she landed on the concrete below. Her husband survived but a large percentage of his body had to have skin grafts; he was in hospital for over a year. Their three sons survived. The lady and her son in the ground floor flat survived unhurt; their flat was hardly damaged.

Here is Mum and Dad's version of that night.

They say they went downstairs to the lady below to have a drink. It seems to be true that it was her wedding anniversary and her husband was away. Apparently they were sitting in her lounge when Mum spotted a reflection of flames in the windows of the blocks of flats behind our house. They all decided to go into the garden to see what was on fire, at the same time hearing the distant wail of sirens as fire engines headed their way. On getting into the garden they at once saw it was our flat on fire. Dad told me they ran to the front of the house; by then the entire street were out and Mum and Dad were hysterical knowing we were trapped inside. Dad also told me he tried to scale the bare walls to the bay window of our bedroom to rescue us, but obviously this was impossible. After this Mum and Dad's recollection of that night is sketchy to say the least. Dad states that the first fire engine arrived and the ladders were not long enough. (We lived on the middle floor of a converted house.) The second fire engine arrived and had no key to access the water pumps or hose, and eventually came the third. The three children on the third floor jumped to safety aided by the firemen but their mother, who was sat on the edge of the roof waiting her turn, panicked, tried to jump and fell to her death as the roof gave way. The man from the top floor was rescued but was nearly baked alive where the intense heat had literally roasted him. Then the firemen eventually got to me and Andrew. We had both stopped breathing and also our hearts had stopped. After a battle of determination I was resuscitated by a neighbour.

59

Andrew was pronounced dead when he arrived at the hospital.

I have tried to confirm the catastrophic events of that night but there are many missing links. My recollections along with what I have been told are like a jigsaw puzzle, where when you fit a piece it looks right but something somewhere tells you maybe another piece was meant to be in that space. The picture is just not quite right.

I have so many unanswered questions. Why did the fire start in two places? Why didn't my parents notice the fire earlier? After all they were only on the floor below, or were they? Did they not hear anything or smell burning until the fire was so established that it was too late? Others had obviously seen and heard the fire because engines were already on their way. There are many versions of that night that have been mentioned over the years; which is the truth? I really don't know, I never will.

Recently, I have been back to the house. When it was suggested that I do this, I was terrified, but I knew I had to do it if only to lay some finality to it all.

The journey from Dorset to London seemed even longer than usual. I hadn't slept the night before. My fitful dozing had been littered by ghosts from the past.

As my husband Martin and I pulled into Wrottesley Road I closed my eyes. I didn't think I could face it, scared of what I might see, what I might remember. I felt the car pull to a halt. The creak of the handbrake being applied confirmed we had stopped. I breathed through my nose to help control the waves of nausea that swept over me; my stomach rolled with each breath I took. A nerve pulsated in my left temple, in rhythm with my racing heart. I gritted my teeth so hard it hurt.

'We're here.' He laid his hand on my bare arm, caressing me gently. He carried on, 'Open your eyes; there's nothing to be scared of.'

I couldn't; my eyelids held as dams to stop the impending flood of tears.

'Come on.' He encouraged me with his soft caring words.

'Turn the car round, drive away.' I was near to hysteria.

'No.' His voice came out strong, stern and determined. 'I'm getting out.'

The click of the handle was followed by the muffled thud of the car door as he closed it behind him. I was alone in solitary silence. The cloak of fear started to feel what it really was, ridiculous, false. There was nothing to be afraid of.

Seconds later I stood beside Martin, holding his hand. The sun shone warmly on my face as I leant back against the car. Shielding my eyes I looked at the house. I let my mind settle as I surveyed what stood before us, what it meant to me, what fear it instilled within me.

It was quite an ordinary house, not big – well, certainly not as big as I remembered it – but not small either. A detached, three-storey, Victorian building, with bay windows; not much else to say, except as I stood there and looked a little more closely, I could see that the decorative mouldings round the middle floor bay window didn't quite match the rest. The bricks at the side and parts of the front of the house, though now weathered, had obviously been replaced. No big sign to show its history but enough for those who know it to see.

I must have stood for ten minutes or more just looking. It was a house, just an ordinary house. In the time I stood there, years of memories, of frozen fear, gently began to melt away. The thaw did not complete; it probably never will. I still get chills running down my spine when I think of that night, but it is certainly a better temperature than if I had never faced the cold at all.

I desperately wanted go to the cemetery to see Andrew's grave. I needed a finality to it all, a chance to say the goodbye I had been so cruelly robbed of by the fire, and by Mum and Dad. They had never taken me to the cemetery, or even told me where it was. Yes, I was young then, maybe they thought it for the best, but this doesn't explain why they never went and, unless I asked, never mentioned Andrew again.

The cemetery was not that hard to find. I had done all the necessary ground work pre-going to London. The man we met at the cemetery office was kind and understanding. He knew we were coming so he had scrolled through years and reams of records to find my brother's entry.

He led us from the cool shadowy office into the bright autumn sun. We walked up the tarmac path that cut between the well-manicured lawns. The odd tree was dotted here and there; I watched as they swayed gently in the breeze. Flower beds cut the carpet of green, producing an array of cheerful colour. I couldn't help but smile. On we walked over the brow of the hill, past the row after row of cream and grey headstones, onward, onward.

'Your brother is buried in a communal grave,' he explained. 'Babies often were in those days.'

'You mean he's not got his own grave?' I questioned.

'No, love; as I say it was quite common in those days. People who couldn't really afford a proper burial, and believe me there were a lot, often had a common ground burial. Your brother is here under this grassy bank.'

We had stopped. A lush green expanse of grass stretched before me.

'Here, I've managed to work out from the records roughly where he will be.' The man was intently looking at a piece of paper. He strode off. 'Come on, this way.' We followed obediently.

'He's there,' I whispered to Martin as I pointed ahead. A patch of buttercups waved their sunny heads in the breeze. I pointed directly at them.

By now I had given up listening to the man, I was sure that was where Andrew had been laid to rest.

'By Lord she's right and all, that's roughly where the nipper will be.'

I stood. Martin and the man discreetly left my side.

'I'll be over here,' Martin whispered as he touched my elbow.

I stood in the stillness; should I kneel? No, I just stood. The breeze had stopped. A small shiver cast goose bumps on my bare arms.

'Hello,' I whispered. 'Hello, Andrew.'

I stared at the ground trying to picture through the soil, through the boxes beneath, trying to imagine how far down he was. Was he at the top or one or two down? Was he at the bottom?

'Where are you?' I whispered.

Suddenly my mind was rushed back at high speed to nearly 40 years earlier. To the day I found out Andrew was never coming back. I felt my legs go from under me and once again I fell to my knees.

'Andrew.' I felt I whispered his name but found out later that I had screamed it.

Emotions that I had successfully locked away after that fateful day so long ago decided that it was time they surfaced. Heart-wrenching sobs shook my body to the core. Years of grief spilled from me and splashed freely onto the grass below. Pounding the ground with my fists, I let out decades of hurt and anger.

Why, why had I let him die? Why did I not do more to save him?

Because you were only six years old, a logical voice whispered inside my head, but I was in no mood to listen to it.

My crying eventually subsided. I realised I was lying on the ground where he was buried. Grass was stuck to my face. My eyes were swollen and hurting, my throat sore and scratchy, my nose running. I sniffed and lifted my face to look for Martin. There he sat on the verge patiently waiting. Not intruding but just being there for when he was needed.

He walked over to where I lay. Kneeling down, he lifted me into his arms and rocked me. He never said a word; he just stroked my hair and rocked me whilst I quietly cried.

I left the cemetery. Before I went we stood together, Martin and I. I knew Andrew would have liked Martin so it was natural for him to stand with me as I said my final goodbyes.

We stood as the autumn afternoon drew to a close. The sun was lower now, throwing the shadows of dancing leaves across the grass, onto the paths and beyond. The buttercups which had waved so merrily earlier were spent, they had begun to close their petals protectively around their delicate hearts, they were ready for rest, and so was I. Just like Andrew I was finally at peace... I was ready to say goodbye, to leave the bad stuff behind buried deep in the brown heavy earth beneath my feet where the shell of Andrew's body lay. I was ready to take the memory of his life with me.

They say the soul makes a person and the body is nothing but a casing to put the soul in. Andrew's soul was now free of that casing. His soul had made him a funny, tormenting, bubbly, gentle, kind little boy who asked for nothing but to be loved, and I will carry on with that love until I take my final breath and beyond.

CHAPTER SEVEN

After the fire Dad moaned constantly, he said that we had to find our own way in life and no one was going to help us. He insisted that we were denied any financial support from the government or any charitable organisations. I was too young to know if this was true.

I do clearly remember going to a big Victorian-style house surrounded by a large garden; it was somewhere in Woolwich, south-east London. We sat in a large high-ceilinged room lined with chairs and waited. A little later a middle-aged woman came in and paraded a variety of clothing before us. We chose from the clothes shown and tried them on. If they fitted we were allowed to keep them. They covered basic requirements. As far as I recall this was roughly what I was allowed: socks two pair, knickers two pair, dress one, cardigan one, coat one, shoes one pair and a nightgown if available. We did this many times throughout my childhood. It was not always the same place but the formalities were identical. We received the clothes, Mum or Dad signed the papers and we left. I now know that this charity organisation was called the WRVS, the Women's Royal Voluntary Service. I am grateful for their input to my life.

This memory alone leads me to believe Dad's rants held little or no substance; they were in fact just more unjustified lies, and we did get help, but he cried wolf hoping for more handouts.

A little while after the fire, Mum disappeared; I had only been home a few short weeks. I woke one morning to find her gone. I wandered aimlessly around the flat where we lived. Dad sat in his chair. I wanted to ask him where she was. You have to understand that it was not just the separation anxiety I developed after the fire that made me so worried, it was also the fact that Mum was never allowed out without Dad unless it was to do something for him. I wanted to ask where she was but I was too scared. Eventually I had no choice, fear and anxiety got the better of me. Dad was sitting in his chair looking out of the window when I entered the front room; he didn't even look at me.

'Dad, where's Mum?' I questioned.

Without moving his gaze he replied. 'You're a big girl now; make your dad a cup of tea.'

'I can't. I don't know how.'

'Well, it's about time you did. You're too bloody mollycoddled, you are; it's about time you grew up.' He turned and looked at me. From his lips tumbled menacing words, cold, harsh, quietly spoken but I knew not to ignore them. 'Now get to the kitchen and make me some tea, like I asked. You wouldn't want to upset me, would you?'

I turned and went to the kitchen.

Untucking a chair from the table I pushed it towards the sink. I knew I had no choice; I had to make the tea. Turning the tap I let the clear cold water rattle its way into the empty kettle, mumbling to myself, '*Please let it be right, please let it be right*.' At just seven years old I successfully made Dad his tea; I also cooked him toast and later some sort of dinner. All the time he sat in his chair. By the time I was allowed to go to bed I still didn't know where Mum was.

The next day saw a change in him. He woke me early.

'Come on my little one, up you get, Dad's going to do you a bit of breakfast, come on.'

He pulled back the blanket that covered me, lifted me from my bed, all the time smiling.

'Off we go then.'

He opened my bedroom door and there in the hallway stood a woman I had never seen before. She looked friendly enough, her young face framed by a tumble of soft but well-controlled curls that ended at her shoulders. I don't remember much else of her appearance apart from her wide smile and warm welcoming eyes.

Still scared by change and unrest I cuddled into Dad. I had no choice; there was no one else to trust. I didn't trust Dad wholly but what else could I do?

'Oh, this is Maggie. Maggie has come to take you to school.' Dad was smiling.

I knew better than to ask questions as he set me down on the floor. When told I obediently washed, dressed, had some food and took Maggie's hand as she led me out onto the street. I did all this in silence. The first thing to hit me was the wide open space of outdoors. Since the fire I had hardly been out and even then never without Mum.

Clinging to Maggie's hand I staggered down the path and grabbed hold of the gate. The traffic thundered by, every car seeming faster and nearer than the last. Someone walked past and lit a match, holding it to the fag in his mouth. To me the innocent flame spelt danger.

Once outside Maggie began a stream of cheerful chatter, asking about my favourite games and if I went to the park much, all the time encouraging me to answer her. I fixed my gaze on the horizon, tightly clenched her hand and did not say a word. Gradually Maggie's chatter died down and all that could be heard was the sound of our footsteps as we walked on.

I had not been to school since the fire. I didn't know if I would go back to my old school or to a new one. It was all too much.

'No, let me go. I want my mum.'

I tried to wriggle my hand away from Maggie's, desperate to get away and run to the safety of my own home.

There was something, something not quite right. Why was Dad being so nice? What was she doing here? Where was Mum?

'I want my mum.' I was hysterical with the fear that had captured me. Nothing was going to soothe me, nothing but the words of Mum.

Maggie stood rooted to the spot, watching me. She then bent to my height.

'OK, OK, we will go home and when I've spoken to your daddy, we will go see your mum, OK?'

Her soothing words stilled me. We went back to the flat. I was left in the front room whilst Maggie and Dad talked. I wanted to cry but decided that I wanted to hear what they were saying more, so I didn't. Though I strained to hear I could only catch the odd word. *Traumatised*, *shock*, *love* and *support* were but a few. I wondered who they were talking about.

True to her word Maggie took me to see Mum. It was an agonising journey but it was worth it. I remember vomiting twice as we walked to the bus stop. The burning bile rested on my tongue long after the sick had gone.

On the bus I knelt on the long seats that sat lengthways, parallel to the bus aisle, and strained my neck to its fullest length so as to get my face as close as possible to the open slit window above me whilst Maggie wrapped her arm tightly round me. I needed to breathe. Little did I know then that was the start of the panic attacks that were going to plague me for a long, long time and occasionally still do.

When we got off the bus I shook so much that my legs wouldn't carry me so Maggie lifted me high into her arms. As she walked she told me about Mum.

'Mummy is in hospital.'

The tingling started somewhere in the pit of my stomach; it lingered there for a while before making its ascent towards my throat. My tongue prickled before going numb. A sledgehammer heartbeat pounded once, hard in my chest. Sounds went distant, I could see Maggie's lips move as she spoke to me but her words were drowned out by the roar that ran through my head. *No more!* I fainted.

A familiar smell crept up my nose, making it wrinkle in disgust. I didn't want to smell it but I still let in a compulsive sniff. Opening my eyes the first thing I saw was Maggie.

'Hey, poppet, you gave me a little scare there.'

'Am I too late?' I asked.

'Are you too late for what?' she queried.

'Is Mum dead yet?'

'No, of course not.'

I had it in my head that everyone I loved that came into hospital died shortly after. As far as I was concerned Mum was no different, she would obviously die.

Mum lay still. Her face so pale blending in with the stiff white sheets tucked and folded crisply under her chin.

'Hello, Anna.'

Mum's words, weak as a kitten's mew, just about reached me. I stood still and watched as she tried to move one of her arms from the tightly tucked bed.

'Shall I help?' I asked. She nodded.

I looked round anxiously for Maggie. I had only known her for a few hours but I already knew I could trust her. She was standing at the far end of the ward with a nurse and doctor; they looked deep in conversation. I turned back to Mum; she had released one of her arms and was beckoning me closer.

'Help me sit up.'

I moved nearer. As she struggled to sit up I caught a glimpse of a bandage wrapped round her arm; a big red tube protruded from it. A wave of understanding came over me.

It was obvious Mum had hurt her arm. I had done that once; I fell off the wall outside our house and took the skin clean off my elbow. It had left a big red crusty scab for ages. I had picked the edges to try to get it off, but all it did was bleed. It was ugly. Dad would call me 'scabby kid'. I hated it.

'Did you fall over?' I asked.

'What?'

'Did you fall over and hurt your arm?' Now I was curious. I moved nearer and lifted the sheets to get a closer look.

'No.' She smiled. 'I didn't. Mummy is not well and has to have some new blood; look.' She pointed to a bag dangling on a pole behind the bed; I hadn't noticed it before. My eyes traced the thick red tube from the bag back to Mum.

'What's wrong with your blood?' I asked, but she didn't reply; she just smiled and asked me how I was.

On the bus journey home I sat on Maggie's lap. I felt safer there.

'What's wrong with Mummy's blood?'

'Nothing.' She smiled. 'Sometimes when people are poorly they need blood to make them better.'

'Where does it come from?' I asked, my curiosity growing.

'Nice healthy people give some of their blood to the hospital, and then the hospital look after it until someone like your mummy needs it.'

I fell silent. I was healthy; perhaps I should give Mum my blood, but how? I hoped I was never ill; I didn't like the thought of anyone else's blood.

Maggie dropped me home and left. Maybe it was being with her that gave me courage, I don't know, but that day I decided to ask Dad why Mum was in hospital. At first he ignored me, but I persisted, asking again and again.

'Dad, why does Mum need new blood? She hasn't hurt herself. Why is she in hospital?' I could see his agitation but

70

I needed to know. I knew I was risking a hiding but I couldn't help it. I still didn't know whether Mum was going to die.

'Make the tea and don't keep questioning me, I'm not a fucking doctor.'

Dutifully I made the tea. Dad sat at the kitchen table and silently watched my every move.

'Bring it in the front room when you've finished,' he grunted.

When I took the tea in to him he was sat in the armchair by the window. The telly was on. He looked at me; his face seemed to have softened.

'Come sit on your dad's lap. I'll tell you all about it.'

Willingly I jumped on his knee, eager to hear what he had to say.

'That's it, come on, sit closer.' He pulled me into him, squirming to get himself comfortable. 'Bloody hell, you're getting a heavy little thing, aren't you?'

'Am I?' I asked. I didn't think I was but maybe he was right.

'You're still my little lap fitter though, aren't you?' He wiggled me about and bounced me up and down.

I knew that familiar look but I deliberately chose to ignore it, instead seized the opportunity to encourage it so I could get my way and ask about Mum.

'Dad.'

'Mmmmm.' His eyes were closed, but I continued.

'Dad, why is Mum in hospital? When will she be home?

'She'll be home soon.'

I continued to fidget whilst talking. 'When's soon?'

He opened his eyes. I could tell by the cold stare that met my gaze that no amount of fidgeting I tried now was going to get him to be nice.

'Get off me, you fucking little whore,' he screamed as he shoved me as hard as he could onto the floor. 'Keep fucking on! You think you can get round me with your play acting, do you? Well you're fucking wrong, you can't. Now fuck off.'

I stood up; defiantly risking everything I answered back.

'I want my mum.'

His gaze held mine for a few seconds that felt like eternity.

'Well if she hadn't got herself knocked up again then she would be here, wouldn't she?'

I didn't know what 'knocked up' meant but I knew I had pushed my luck too far already; I decided to leave it there.

In later years I found out that Mum had been pregnant. She had a miscarriage that went wrong and had a severe infection. She had nearly died but thank God didn't. After a while she returned home and things returned to our family's version of reality.

CHAPTER EIGHT

Somewhere between living at Wrottesley Road, the fire and Mum having her miscarriage, she gave birth to another baby.

I don't recall her even being pregnant. I was certainly never told to expect another baby brother or sister.

The information I have is vague, and I can't throw any truthful light on this because I just don't have any recollection of him. I must have been denied his existence because as you have already gathered I have many vivid memories of my childhood. If I had known him I most certainly would have remembered him.

I know his name was Raymond. He was born on 28 June 1966. Allegedly he never came home from hospital; he was too ill. He died on 20 July, less than one month after he was born. On the death certificate it states bronchial pneumonia and a laryngeal stridor.

I deliberated over adding this information purely because it is so limited, but my belief is every child, no matter how short their life is, deserves recognition. Raymond deserves to be in this story because he was and is a part of my past. I may not have known him but he was still my brother, and though they chose to forget he was still my parents' son. Just because they pay no respect to the memory of him, doesn't mean he didn't exist. He was a soul. He lived and breathed if only for a short while. Maybe considering the past up until then, and the future that was about to happen, it was as well that God took him home when he did. He would probably not have survived the following years.

Though I have difficulty understanding Mum's view of all that happened I cannot help but have a deep sadness within. Between the years of 1958 and 1966 my parents lost four sons, two within a few months of each other. Because of his ways my dad's hardened exterior was and is easier to understand, but Mum? She must have been broken, even if she has never admitted it. The only way I can soften to her is to imagine that sometimes in her quiet moments she remembers the babies and maybe sheds a tear. I think this is just my fanciful imagination rather than the truth.

CHAPTER NINE

It has been a few years since I decided to write my story. It happens in fits and starts, some days writing until my eyes ache and my fingers falter, others leaving the pages untouched. Across the whole journey it has been a healing process. An acceptance of the level of abuse I sustained has been reached. I had to read what had happened for it to be able to sink in. The lack of acknowledgement from my mother for all these years that bore into my soul is also a type of abuse. I have constantly questioned for years if what I was subjected to as a child was that bad... Of course it was! Mentally, physically and sexually abused, but it was only when the mashed-up words spilled among my tears onto the page and they lay in black and white for me to read that I could really accept the situation for what it was and is.

They say that one in five adults were abused as children. It is an impossible statistic to ascertain, partly because who determines what is abuse and what is not and partly because of the shame and guilt that surrounds the victims which often imprisons them to a life of secrecy.

After the hours I have spent on these pages, if one person who reads them can be released then the content has been worth writing.

So I became a country girl just as Dad said I would, living in a string of cottages tied to his job and safe as a home as long as Dad kept working, which was as often as... never.

There were many wealthy families throughout the Kent countryside looking for house-keepers, gardeners or handymen. Most jobs came with a rent-free cottage so whenever Dad was too lazy to continue to work and got the sack, or he just got itchy feet, with a little of his charm and buckets full of lies we were able to move on to the next place without too much trouble.

School was a distant memory occasionally brought to the fore by an eager school board man knocking at one or another of our many front doors. I would be dragged reluctantly to a village school. Usually this was a house that the head teacher lived in but the front rooms were used as classrooms. I would sit an oddball in among the children of varying ages. They would not talk to me, and I not to them. Aged eight or nine I knew it was a waste of time to have friends. I wasn't going to be there long enough to forge relationships of any worth so there was no point. No, my friends were in other places.

One of the houses we lived in was on 'Charrington's Fruit Farm'. I can't remember where in Kent it was or how long we stayed there; certainly not a year, more likely to be six months or less.

The cottage was a semi set off a farm track opposite a pond. Dad wanted to fish in the pond; he told me there was a massive pike he wanted to catch. He never did fish; I don't know why. The long thin back garden trailed down to a stream which bordered the orchards and fields beyond. The stream was my sanctuary. Warm summer days were spent plunging my feet into its cool waters, pressing against the wet stones whilst ripples danced between my toes. I sat patiently still, awaiting the appearance of tiny mammals which lived in and on the muddy banks, watching dragonflies flitting dipping their tails, tiny fish anxiously darting from bank to bank looking for something they had lost. I was rewarded well; these creatures knew all my troubles. When times were good they knew all my joys.

There my fantasy world could develop. I would muse, sing, draw in the dirt, but most I would pretend I had no mum and dad and I was always happy. Simple childlike thoughts clouded with the contrast of reality.

I was brought up being alone; it didn't bother me. If I hungered, rather than go inside, where there was little more than bread if I was lucky, I would walk down the track toward the derelict oast-houses where the long wooden packing sheds stood. Opening the swing doors, leaving the bright afternoon filled with bird song, I would enter a world of dimmed cool production lines. Once my eyes adjusted to this new muted light I was on the search. Women stood in rows flanking waist-high rollers that shifted the recently picked apples along, in front of scrutinising eyes, toward the square boxes lined with diamond-shaped grids that held the precious fruit. Bad, bruised and blemished were seized and delivered by swift hands to the nearby swill bin. Some did not get that far; some fell wayside and into my waiting arms.

The balmy days of autumn played their coloured symphony for many weeks; I spent them escaping. Jumping on the back of the tractor trailer as it trundled past our house toward the fruit-filled orchards to lose myself among the traveller kids that came with their families to work on the farm at harvest time. On sunny days I helped pick fruit, played chase, ducking under low-slung branches, swinging round warm bark trunks. On rainy days all the adults would either stay in the caravans that arrived with them or work in the packing sheds; us kids would disappear, pockets filled with fruit, into the large greenhouses. Sitting on straw-strewed floors, listening to the rain thundering against the glass, we were warm and dry. I still love the smell of a tomato-filled greenhouse; it's homely to me, filling me with warm memories and comforting satisfaction.

It was one of my saddest times when the late autumn days took on a distinctive chill and the travellers left; I recall begging them to take me with them but of course they couldn't.

The ladies in the packing shed took to me, one in particular; she told me she had once been a traveller and there was no life like it. She showed me things that made me smile like mice with long shaggy coats that lived in the cooler room, how to make apples sweeter with the juice from Nasturtiums, how to crush lavender against your skin to make perfume. I don't recall her name but her kindness softened the both physical and mental blows that I received.

It was whilst living at Charrington's that two major things dawned on me. One, that actually Dad was not at all nice at times; the other, that I wasn't sure he even loved me. What brought to light this harsh reality? I was given a comic by one of the women that worked in the packing sheds. In the comic was a drawing competition; after much waiting for the right moment to approach Mum and Dad, I persuaded them to let me enter. I tore a blank leaf from a book to act as my page and sketched the daffodil field in pencil. I told the lady who gave me the comic what I was doing and she brought in coloured pencils that belonged to her children for me to borrow. I sent the drawing off and weeks later I received a letter to say I had won first prize, a bike! Even Dad congratulated me and arrangements were made to pick up my prize from the railway station where it was being delivered. On the day it was due to arrive Dad wouldn't let me go with him to collect it; he said I was too excited so would be too much bother. When he left I found my place leaning on the front gate and waited for his return. I had never had a bike or any other brand new toy of my own. I must have got on Mum's nerves when insistently questioning what was taking Dad so long. At first she laughed but as dusk fell I could sense she became anxious.

Hours later I still stood at the gate defying the dark to scare me into going indoors. 'He's here, Mum, he's coming.' My squeals of delight echoed down the darkened lane.

'I waited all fucking afternoon for your fucking bike, half my fucking day wasted.' His harsh words accompanied a sharp slap to the back of my head.

'Well?' Mum questioned as Dad entered the house with me trailing behind.

'No fucking bike, I could have been doing better stuff than waiting around for her.'

'Smells like you have.' Mum smelt what I did: stale beer and fags as Dad stumbled to the nearest chair.

'Fuck off.'

Mum ushered me to bed with no mention of dinner.

'Be for the best, we will speak to 'im in the morning when 'e's in a better mood.'

I did as I was told. With a heavy heart I crawled into my bed; too sad to cry and tired from the hours stood at the gate, I slept.

Hours later I was woken by raised voices. It didn't faze me, I was used to it, but tonight as at times before I lay and listened. The first words I heard were...

'You bastard, you know how much she wanted that bike. What's fucking wrong with you? What evil father sells his kid's toys?'

I can't remember what followed but I remember hearing that Mum hadn't got the money she had promised. From things I learnt and heard in future, the conversation probably went something like this.

'Oh yes you, you stupid cow, couldn't even get 'im 'ere to give you money today, could you? He didn't want your rotting fanny, did 'e?'

'Shut up, you know 'e was busy, but that's still not good enough reason to sell 'er bike, is it? It ain't the first time we would 'ave gone without, is it? At least Anna would be happy.'

'You trying to say I don't provide for my family? Shut up...'

I didn't want to hear the rest, I had heard enough. I held the pillow over my head to block out the battle going on in the other room. The feathers muffled my ears but the words repeating over and over in my head could not be silenced... *'You didn't have to sell 'er bike, did you?'* But he had. I buried my head further into the suffocating feathers. I wondered what it would feel like to leave it there.

Another thing I realised was that my Uncle Harry must be a very nice man. He lived quite a way away but came to visit regularly, sometimes once or even twice a week. Whenever he came he would call me 'his lovely'. ''Ello my lovely,' he would say with a grin. Mum would make him tea. I used to get pretty upset because every time he came Dad would always find something for me to do which meant I had to go out. I missed my time with my uncle and was quite jealous of the fact Mum got to stay in with him on her own. Uncle Harry always left us £5 and Mum would always cook a nice dinner that night. Little did I know the Uncle Harry I liked so much I would learn to hate with more vengeance and bitterness than I ever knew possible.

The man that had lived in the top flat of the house where we had had the fire came to visit us a few times whilst we lived at Charrington's; his name was Kenneth. I knew Mum had spent a lot of time visiting him whilst he spent a year or so in hospital so they had forged a friendship. I was scared when he visited; he was covered in scars on his face, hands and arms from skin grafts. Dad didn't seem to mind him coming.

The few years of country life were dotted with the accepted amount of beatings that had become part of my normal days. Food became bountiful or non-existent, never consistent. Bailiffs came; bags packed, we trudged from halfway houses to bedsits. We lived where we landed. In Kent this was Wateringbury, Matfield, Cranbrook,

Maidstone and a few other places I can't remember the name of, but it was never long before city smoke filled my lungs again.

Big Nan often took us in; we would make the long journey back to London and live a sort of half-life sleeping on her living room floor until something better came up. I was ecstatic to see her and she me. She would say, ''Ere, come and count my buttons, I've been saving 'em for you.' A large biscuit tin would emerge and the contents would be tipped out onto the cloth-covered table. I would count the buttons into piles, shiny, non-shiny, red, pink and blue, and my favourite: the sparkly ones. Inevitably the clatter of the buttons annoyed Dad and I would have to stop. Big Nan would 'tut tut' at him and mutter something under her breath; I could never hear what but I would give a good guess it wasn't pleasant. She would then, weather permitting, take me into the communal garden to make daisy chains.

Night after night I slept in the single bed with Big Nan, cuddled and safe, whilst Mum and Dad slept on the floor, but eventually the news I hated came, always delivered the same way.

'We're moving to a new house tomorrow; ain't your dad clever, he got you a new home.' He would puff out his chest and smile. My reaction was always the same: on the outside a smile and jump for joy. On the inside a leaded sadness fell into the pit of my stomach.

It was after one of these sessions that we moved into Brent Road. Our country days were over for a while as we settled back in London. As I waved goodbye to Big Nan I knew my few weeks of respite were at an end and another new beginning, another new chapter was about to start.

CHAPTER TEN

Brent Road was in south-east London, once an affluent area filled with grand detached Victorian houses, skirted with greenery and tall trees. The trees still remained standing tall and straight though now the grass at their feet was long and unkempt; the majority of the houses were now divided into flats, bedsits and rooms; the ornate regal porches and sturdy front doors were now decorated with an array of bell pushes underlined with the words *Flat A*, *Flat B*, *Flat C* or whatever fitted.

The house we moved into was no different to the rest; it had once been grand but now peeling paint and cracked windows reflected the standard of the rooms within.

We had one room at the back of the house, on the ground floor, overlooking the long-overgrown garden. We shared a cubby-hole kitchen and a dingy toilet with the others that lived on the same floor. There was no bathroom. Our only source of hot water was to boil a kettle, which was adequate as long as we had money to feed the meters that gave us electricity and gas.

Dad was a stickler for cleanliness; not a day would go by without us all having a strip wash. A bowl would be filled with water, hot or cold depending, and I would be sponged down head to toe.

Winter mornings I would lie under the sheets and stuff my feet into the cold corners of my bed whilst listening to the wake-up noises of our room: Mum going out to the kitchen, the kettle whistling, and Dad calling her to hurry up whilst he sat up in bed and waited. She would return, take the bowl full of stale urine that had accumulated overnight and empty it down the loo. These noises would help me to decide if and when I made my presence known. If Dad sounded angry I would lie quiet, if he sounded happy I would sit up and smile... In my routine, I knew how to behave to avoid being a nuisance. When he was happy Dad would throw back the covers and let me crawl in bed with him, inviting me into his warm intimate space just to hug me. I would sit with him and sip tea whilst Mum did the morning necessities to get ready for the day.

Whilst living at Brent Road Dad as always worked tirelessly on tidying and cultivating the garden. No one minded as none of the other tenants, a mixture of drop-outs, unfortunates and drug users, could be bothered. His efforts were noticed, and it wasn't long before an admiring passer-by offered him a job as their gardener.

Things ticked along, and once again an acceptable level of existence reigned.

Kenneth, the man who lived in the house where we had the fire some three years before, visited a lot, usually when Dad was at work. Mum insisted I call him Uncle Kenneth; I did as I was asked, though I didn't see why I should as he wasn't my uncle at all, not like Uncle Harry who really was my uncle as he was married to Mum's sister. Dad asked Kenneth once in an angry voice why he never came when he was home; Kenneth said because he was a lorry driver and he would sneak off work to visit us and it just clashed with the times Dad worked. Dad mumbled his acceptance, backing down from the plainly obvious because he was too much of a coward to confront him; instead if Dad returned from work to find Kenneth had been he would scream abuse at Mum, stripping the bed and checking the sheets, looking for head dents on the pillows. Mum would take the wrath almost with acceptance.

Uncle Harry used to visit a lot as well, coming a few times a week though always when Dad was home. He would come in; ''Ello my lovely,' he would say with a twinkle in his eyes. I would beam him a smile; knowing that we were going to eat well that night made me happy. The only thing that saddened me about his visits was that since we had moved into our room at Brent Road whenever he came Dad would insist on going out for a walk with me. It made me cross; I wanted to spend time with Uncle Harry who was always so nice.

Brent Road was the place of some of my better memories... Sitting on the front wall watching the sun set, collecting snails, making dens among the tall weeds at the end of the back garden, having my very first ever pet, a rabbit which Dad named Whisky, settling into Foxhill Junior School and attending two or three times a week. I had the most wonderful teacher, Mr Mortimer; he believed in me and helped me believe in myself. I will forever remember that remarkable man.

The attic at Brent Road was occupied by a man Dad called 'Creeping Jesus'. A quiet polite character of few words, but an obvious gentle spirit, whose real name was John.

John always had a smile for me; on his way out he would often sneak me a biscuit or a sweet. I liked John but never more-so than Christmas morning when opening the door to a quiet knock revealed him standing there with a shiny coach-style doll's pram. Excitement overwhelmed me, my squeals of delight echoing into adult ears. John beamed. Dad joined me at the door.

'What's this, John? A bit extravagant for her, I think.' He nodded his head toward me as he spoke.

John's smile clouded over.

'Saw it on the waste ground, that's all, did it up a bit, thought she might like it.'

John's dark eyes locked in battle with Dad's insipid blues. Silence strangled the festive air whilst the two men clashed. My hand dropped from the handlebars of my precious gift as Dad pulled me away, tucking me behind him.

'Very kind of you, John, I am sure she likes it.'

With one swift action the pram was dragged into the room and the door firmly shut in John's face. Not another word was said about the toy that though I had no doll became my object of affection for many months. The pram disappeared when we moved: lost, Dad said.

CHAPTER ELEVEN

The difficulty in writing this is that revisiting the memories raises such raw emotions. It is unexplainable how the pain remains buried deep inside and yet to the outside world I seem a level-headed well-balanced individual.

I wrote this story for many reasons but the main one was to raise awareness that mental abuse can be just as harmful as physical abuse. The ammunition of insecurity and fear can crash through the walls of your defence and slaughter your stability, breaking it down into useless rubble. It is the most natural thing after having your defences blown apart to build them higher and stronger, effectively keeping yourself from harm but also at times keeping out the people and things that really matter. Sometimes wounds don't heal under plasters or dressings; they just need to be exposed to the fresh air. There is no reason for your past to shape your future, and I am living proof of that, living proof that if you take down the walls willingly and let the right people in at the right moments your life can not only change but flourish and bloom into the beautiful thing it is meant to be.

My memories of abuse and suffering, although unacceptable, are often accompanied by a longing. That longing is for the glimpses of what I can only call true affection that, though far and few between, did exist between my parents and me; it isn't easy but it is well worth it.

Much of my life was spent travelling a road of confusion between love and sex as is often the case for victims of sexual abuse. I chased affection of a sexual kind, tripping in and out of relationships and affairs, none of which satisfied my longing for *true love*. It was only when I relinquished the unfounded hate and guilt that I had for myself that I rediscovered the meaning of *love*, for myself and others.

Even though I know I was abused physically I cannot really accept that before the age of nine I was sexually abused in any way. Reading what I have already written you may well disagree, but the fact is I myself cannot recall many memories that are cut and clear to be sexual abuse. One thing I am now comfortable with accepting, though, is that my childhood was far from acceptable.

Brent Road changed me. As many children of the sixties and seventies I was often found playing alone outside. The difference between then and now is clear; if Mum and Dad were pre-occupied I was left in my innocence to wander. I would go to the end of the road and sit on the pavement and in my head escape to a different world. A world of love and laughter, a world where parents played with their children, hugged them, a world where the slaps and punches didn't exist, the fights, the arguments disappeared and I was happy, a world where I had a permanent home and food in my belly... a world like my friends at school seemed to have.

One day around dusk I sat on the pavement at the end of the road playing with a couple of snails I had found; a man stopped in a car. He asked me if I was lost, I said no, he asked me what I was doing, I told him about my snails, he got out of his car to see them. When he sat down beside me he put his hand on my knee, I got scared and told him I had to go. He pushed me backwards on the ground and put his hand up my dress and into my knickers. I screamed and he let me go. Jumping into his car he drove away. Now I guess I had a lucky escape; then I was just scared and ran home.

Later that night I told Mum, she told Dad, he beat me and called me a whore.

School was my safety, my sanctuary. Considering I had had little schooling previous to this time, I blossomed. It turned out I was bright and eager to learn. I tried hard not to miss too many days, and for the first time in my life I began to stand up to Dad if he said I couldn't go.

One day despite feeling ill I argued I wanted to go to school; eventually I won the battle but I was so ill that the school nurse sent me home. It wasn't like today where your parents would get a call to come and collect you; few people had phones; there was no way of contacting Mum and Dad so I was sent off home alone.

The walk home took eternity; by the time I arrived I virtually crawled to the door.

Our house had a large wooden front door which usually stayed unlocked during the day; inside that were the doors to all our rooms which also had individual locks. I slumped against the external door, my body aching, my head spinning. The door stuck, no matter how I tried I couldn't open it... it was locked. Though hazy confusion I noticed a lorry parked outside, I knew that Kenneth had come to visit Mum, my heart momentarily lifted; she must be home. I sat down on the step as I banged on the door calling Mum through my tears; I threw up. No answer. I needed to make Mum hear but no matter how I tried she didn't answer. Dragging my aching body, delirious with fever, I struggled round to the back of the house to bang on the window. The window was high up and I could just about see over the wide stone sill.

'Mum,' I cried, now just audible. I could just see through the murky window; she was there, lying on her bed. Uncle Kenneth was lying on top of her.

I banged on the glass as hard as I could. The man's head was buried in her neck as she turned her attention to me; a startled look fleetingly crossed her face before she turned away.

I made my way back to the front of the house expecting her to run to the door; she didn't... blackness descended as my knees gave way.

I returned to the day lying on my bed; Mum was holding my hand. Uncle Kenneth had gone to be replaced by a figure I didn't know.

'Hello, I am a doctor. Gave your mum quite a fright there, you did. You should have tried to knock on the door.'

'I found her on the front step, didn't even know she was there.' Mum's voice echoed through the darkness that threatened to descend.

Liar, I silently screamed. *You saw me.* I was too weak for the words to come.

It turned out I had mumps; a severe reaction caused it to last the whole of summer.

During the time I was recovering we moved, this time to a newly built tower block of flats right over the road from my school. We must have lived there a while because I recall the summer of the following year and still living there when I experienced one of the mentally cruellest acts Dad had ever performed; the memory is so engraved that the sinking disappointment it caused still haunts me.

'Want a birthday party?'

The question rendered me speechless.

'Well answer your dad then, do you want one or not?'

'Yes please,' I answered, fully expecting him to say *'Well you can't have one'* and then laugh, but he didn't. He said I could. I was ecstatic; I had never been allowed anything so extravagant. My birthday was usually virtually ignored.

There were a few weeks left until we broke from school for the summer holidays. Dad let Mum help me make some invites. Because I had been at Foxhill School for a year or more I had made friends. It was a deprived area and though bullying was still a problem I fought my corner and earned respect by doing so.

My friend Anne and I were particularly close; she was what I would class as my best friend. We sat on hot tarmac in the sun-filled playground planning the party. I was so excited; it sounds selfish but I knew the ten people that were coming were likely to bring me presents.

On the night before we broke from school I eagerly packed the invitations into my satchel.

''Ere, before you do that show me them then.' Dad's eyes sparkled igniting my excitement even more.

I pulled them from my satchel and handed them over. He turned them over and over in his brown hairy hands, looking from them to me. His smile encouraged me to shuffle forward and lean on his knee. Dropping all my defences I talked freely about the party; he nodded over and over.

'Go get Mum to make a cuppa, will you?'

Happily I skipped away, my footsteps as light as my mood. On return I added the invitations to the contents of my satchel. At school the next day I handed out invites along with goodbyes. We were all moving on to secondary school, most to Plumstead Manor. My parents had not spoken of it so I had no idea where I was going. There was sadness inside, a sixth sense that told me after my party I may never see my friends again.

Anne and I met frequently throughout summer; her dad had a car and often brought her over but I was never allowed to hers.

The morning of my party dawned. I hardly slept the night before. Dad's enthusiasm only seeded my flourishing excitement. Mum busied herself making food. There was little of it but Anne's dad had given us jelly.

Anne and her dad arrived ten minutes early. He brought a cut-out pin the tail on the donkey and toilet rolls. We never had toilet roll, we always used scrunched newspaper or washed ourselves. The relief I felt at such a small gesture was enormous. I hadn't thought of how much I would be ridiculed without loo roll. Anne's dad was a kind thoughtful man; I am sorry that over the years we have all lost touch.

The time ticked on. Three pm, the start time, came and went; we sat. 3.10, 3.20, where was everyone? Dad sat grinning, in unusually good humour. No one came.

Anne's dad picked her up as planned; Mum spoke to him about what had happened.

'I'm not surprised, Anne's invite had no address on; if the others didn't probably no one knew where you lived.'

I watched Mum's face pale before she quickly composed herself and saw Anne and her dad out. Mum knew as well as I did all the invites including Anne's had the address carefully printed on the bottom. It was the only bit Mum had insisted she write; she said it had to be legible so people knew where to come. Closing the door she turned to look at Dad.

'Do you know anything about what he just said?'

'Not me, love.' He shrugged his shoulders and raised his hands, his face expressionless.

The next day Anne showed me her invite; the bottom had been torn off, her dad was right, and there was no address.

Dad never admitted that the night he looked at the invites he destroyed the address so no one would come, but by his reaction both Mum and I knew the answer. I never had the chance to find out because just as predicted I didn't get to Plumstead Manor as once again we were on the move, and I was going to grow up faster than I ever imagined.

CHAPTER TWELVE

I was 11; we were living back in the countryside near a little village called Wateringbury. Dad had landed yet another tied job working for the owner of a well-known estate agent's, managing a private country estate which consisted of manicured gardens, fruit orchards and a grand house. Mum did the cleaning. In return apart from wages we got to live rent-free in a beautiful chocolate-box cottage with open fires, quirky rooms and lattice windows.

When we first moved in I didn't attend school, I was left to wander freely round the grounds and explore. Eventually the school board man caught up with us and I was put through my 11+ exam to assess which school I should attend. Amazingly I passed with enough marks to go to grammar school. I was elated.

As I lay in bed that night dreams of becoming a writer, a vet, a doctor, anything I wanted floated through my mind, hardly interrupted by the roar of anger that crashed through the wall that separated my bedroom from Mum and Dad's.

The next morning we walked the five or so miles to a block of offices to see the lady who had sat with me whilst I took my 11+.

Once again I found myself in the same room. The view from the third floor office distracted me. I wriggled my bum back in the metal-framed chair until my legs stuck out like sticks poking from under my too short skirt. Mum and Dad sat either side of me.

'She won't be going to any grammar school.'

The words banged into me, knocking me away from my musings and back into the room.

'Nope, no posh grammar, she ain't that type. She'd be unhappy. Me and 'er mum agree, don't we love?' Dad's hand rested on Mum's knee. From where I was sitting I could see his cruel fingertips biting into her flesh; white patches of pressure edged with angry red were growing around the skin trapped by his fingers

I looked at Mum, perched uncomfortably on the edge of her seat, hands folded in her lap. *Look up, Mum, look at me*, my eyes screamed beseechingly; my lips stayed sealed.

'Mr Carter, I am sure Anna would benefit greatly if she were to attend.'

'No, she doesn't need no stuck up education. I never 'ad it and look at me. I did well for myself and my family.' He puffed out his chest, looking at us both with his bitter eyes that defied us to say any different.

The lady continued to argue my corner to no odds. Watching me avidly she must have seen my face fall as Dad had clearly laid down the rules that none of us, not even she, would dare to disobey. But there was something: she questioned and sympathised, even agreed with Dad; why? It turned out she played him at his own game. OK, I couldn't go to grammar, but she told Dad if he let me go to technical college we would be entitled to a grant for school uniform and shoes. Not surprisingly with ££ signs flashing in his eyes, he agreed.

The grant came and disappeared before I knew anything about it, though I did get new shoes from a voucher spent in Clarks.

Having no uniform made a difficult time at tech virtually unbearable. I clearly remember the oversized brown and yellow floral dress I had to wear every day. There was plenty of bullying from the pupils concerning my stupid dress, pointing, giggling, going on about me being poor. I could put up with that; I was used to being the odd one out, but the humiliation from some of the teachers was a different matter. I think many gave up on me. The usual intermittent attendance coupled with lack of uniform made my fitting in near on impossible. If I wanted to go to school Dad would say no; if I didn't he would force me to, making Mum frogmarch me to the gates. I started to play ill in school to get sent home, returning to the sickbay time and time again faking headaches and stomach aches. Eventually the nurse got wise and told me to lie down rather than go home; it was then I stepped up a gear. Waiting until after lunch I would save a little food. In the lesson I would sneak food into my mouth and chew and chew it into a pulp, then proceed to pretend to spontaneously vomit. The girls would scream and the sight would get me immediate dismissal to the nurse and consecutively home.

Why, I ask myself, did I want to go home with all its trappings? But home for me was time to disappear and become another person, wandering the orchards and the gardens. It was on one of these occasions whilst up in the top orchard that the owner of the estates saw me.

It was a dull day in May; the winds still cool against my skin, the threat of rain hanging in a grey sagging sky. I was watching the chickens peck-pecking away when his voice broke into my solace.

'What are you doing here?' His plummy accent, strange to my ears, made it hard for me to understand him; therefore I was a little scared.

'Just watching, sir.' I didn't know this man at all but I knew he was very rich; I thought maybe he was related to the queen. (He wasn't.)

The soft wrinkles that dressed his face deepened as his eyebrows rose. 'Are you frightened of me?' His voice carried surprise.

'No, sir,' I murmured back. Was he going to hurt me, or touch me down there in a secret place? We were alone. My heart hammered in my chest; the fear must have been evident. He stepped back as if sensing my terror.

'Do you like books?' he asked. 'I've seen you up here before, sitting reading. Why don't you come to the house? I'll lend you some books that belonged to my children when they were young. Come on.' He held out his hand; I hesitated, but something in his eyes spelt *trust me, it's OK*. A gentle warmth and softness wrapped around my hand as I placed mine in his.

'Your mum's at the house, no need to be afraid.'

'Is Dad?'

'No, he's working elsewhere.'

The curtain of fear fell in swathes and my footsteps trod it into oblivion as I followed to the big house.

I spent the afternoon cross-legged in a large high-ceilinged room. A fire burned in the grate, books scattered around me. I was allowed to take a few of the books back home with me, a set of four called *The World of Children*. I was delighted a few years ago when I found the same set of books during a trawl round a boot fair; I bought them for a bargain price of £4 and treasure them to this day.

It is hard to believe how my life has changed. I am writing this chapter early on a Saturday morning, sat outside my favourite café called 'Flirt' in Bournemouth. It is mid-summer. The people sitting around me leisurely drinking coffee have no idea what I am writing; some are obviously curious… many writers come here so I feel comfortable.

Borrowing books from the big house became a habit that carried me through the long hot summer of 1972. In August came my birthday; it was now usually acknowledged by Mum and Dad, a card sometimes, a 'happy birthday', if Dad had a job I would get my favourite meal of pork chop and spaghetti, to make it extra special the pork chop would have a kidney in, but I never expected and rarely got any

95

presents. Dad would always say that he would get me something when he had money, but up until that year I don't remember ever receiving presents. This is not to say I didn't, I just don't remember.

1972 was different; Mum came back from cleaning up at the big house with a carefully wrapped parcel. ''Ere, they got you a birthday present.'

Dad was fuming.

''Ow do they know it's 'er birthday? You been telling them our business?'

'No I ain't, they're just being nice, that's all, no 'arm in it.'

I sat quiet, longing for the parcel but dared not ask.

'Suppose they got it 'cause you're fucking around with the Mrs up there, you fucking Brillo-pad rubber.'

I didn't understand.

'Ow, fuck off Dick, you don't know what the fuck you're talking about.'

'I seen you at the window, upstairs in 'er bedroom, you fucking lesbo.'

The row had started; it was my fault; if I hadn't gone to the big house this wouldn't be happening. I sat quiet and soaked in all the information being thrown round the room. Thoughts crashed crazily round my confused mind. How could I escape? I knew if I moved from the place I stood I would attract Dad's attention and he would turn on me. I stood as still as I could; it didn't work.

'This is all your fucking fault, it's that stuck-up crowd you mix with at that school. Think you're better than me, do you? Well you're fucking not.'

'Don't start on her, Dick, she ain't done nothing.'

'Don't side with 'er, it's 'er fault!'

His eyes burned into me; hot fire of fear ran through me; I knew I wasn't going to escape. The beating was no worse than usual. With my arms across my face and head I took it; Mum stood and watched helpless to stop him.

Hours later with an empty belly I lay in my cold lonely room. The row had stopped.

A few weeks later Dad took it into his head that the house was haunted. He claimed he had seen things in their bedroom; he looked genuinely scared. Among protest from both me and Mum their bed was moved to the lounge and my mattress was put on the floor beside it. He said he was protecting us, he heard that of the last two families that had lived there the man had become ill and one had even died. He was convinced the alleged haunting had something to do with it.

Ironically Dad did become ill, not his usual faked sickness, but really ill. I don't know what was wrong but he went to hospital several times. He didn't die, he got better, but by then he was lapping up the deserved attention and proceeded to play up his illness, claiming it was more than just temporary and he was far too ill to go back to work.

Opposite where we lived was Mote Park, a beautiful oasis of rolling grassy banks surrounding a large lake where you could fish or take out a rowing boat. Mum still worked at the big house. Dad re-ignited his passion for fishing. He got a mail order catalogue and ordered all the equipment. Most days although supposedly too ill for work he would be found in the park fishing; he insisted I go with him as I would enjoy it and to some degree I did, though after the first time I caught something he raged so badly with jealousy that he threw my rod into the lake. It then became a battle... every time we went should I tackle up wrong so the fish couldn't bite, or should I risk catching something and encounter another blow or torrent of rage? Either way I couldn't win.

I got used to sleeping on the mattress. I learnt to block out the noises of sex that took place. It would always start the same, Dad's persuasive voice cajoling Mum, convincing her I was asleep or wouldn't hear and even if I did I wouldn't understand. He would ask her to do certain things like stroke or kiss his cock or talk about his fingers inside her. Sometimes he would be angry and force her into it.

Every night at 10 pm Dad would watch the news, wind up the alarm clock, get a glass of water and the washing-up bowl to piss in through the night. The toilet was in the back porch and he refused to go out there in the dark.

One particular night I had a nightmare; I had them often, always the same dream. I would be in a dark room filled with a swirling mist, screaming to get out, banging on walls, windows and doors. Just as I felt I could not breathe I would wake up breathless and crying. Dad had been in a good mood all day. When I woke screaming he let Mum crawl over him and get out of bed to comfort me.

'Bring 'er in 'ere, Barb, I'll give her a cuddle.'

Mum returned to bed and I crawled gladly into Dad's arms.

'Shuffle in, pet,' he invited. I lay against him, Mum on one side and me on the other. He spooned into me as I burrowed deeper into the covers. I could feel the hardness growing in his groin area, pressing through his pyjamas. There was a familiarity about this feeling, I didn't know why; it made me feel comfortable and loved so I stayed there.

It became a natural thing for me to sleep with my parents, spooned in security, Dad's cock pressing against me. My nightmares subsided; I felt safe.

It was around this time I started to explore myself again, often touching my private parts, getting excitement followed by gratification, followed by a comforting and secure feeling. I didn't think it was bad or wrong. On the few occasions I was caught and told off, I had a distant guilt, but the majority of the time I was happy to do it. It became a daily thing; when I was alone I would touch my most intimate parts until I felt better, more relaxed, calmer. It was just another escape route but also the beginning of a much deeper confusion of 'sex equals love' playing a major role in my life.

Eventually the boss got fed up with Dad's behaviour and he was sacked. We had to leave our home and returned to London to once again live with Big Nan. Whilst packing up our possessions I found the present that I had never opened on my birthday. Carefully I unwrapped the paper to reveal a green hard cover stamped in silver, *The Children of the Bells*: poems for children. I hid the book among my things. It was a lifeline to me from an adult that had compassion and understood my love for reading. Some 40 or so years later that book still lives on my shelf. Occasionally I take it down and flick through the well-thumbed pages.

I question: what was abuse in the sixties and seventies? What is the definition? Contrary to today your parents, neighbours, teachers and even the local policeman on the beat were allowed to clip your ear or deal out physical punishment if they felt justified. Sexual abuse I have no doubt was rife, swept under the carpet by an oppressed society recovering from a battle-worn country. One of the problems I have in writing my story is that the abuse of then and now, whilst maybe similar, are viewed very differently. If then I had told of Dad's actions of violence, how much would have been questioned and how much classed as acceptable? Was it acceptable to sleep with your parents? Many brothers and sisters of ages similar to mine shared beds. What level you class my abuse at is for you to decide. As my childhood moved on the worst of the definite physical, mental and sexual abuse was yet to come.

CHAPTER THIRTEEN

We moved back to London, and after a short spell of staying with Big Nan the council offered us a place to live. We had the top two floors of an old Victorian semi in Manthorpe Road, Plumstead. It was what was classed as a halfway house, in other words temporary accommodation until the council could find us something more permanent. I didn't care that it was in a state or temporary.

We moved our few possessions in. Without question all the bedroom furniture got put in the lounge; my bed against one wall, Mum and Dad's against the other. The TV was put in the recess of the big bay window. The room reminded me of Wrottesley Road; in my reoccurring nightmares I relived the fear of being trapped in the fire. Once I woke Mum and Dad by screaming. I screamed louder when the heavy hand landed hard against my skull, bringing the night sky stars into the room to dance in the space surrounding me. I learnt the hard way that night; all future dreams were cried out into my pillow.

To me, even though I was a country girl at heart, the move back to the area was a welcome one; it meant I could go to Plumstead Manor School with all my old friends from Foxhill, and sure enough that is what I did.

Many of my old friends were in different classes, ranked by ability; the intimacy of a small primary school was lost in a sea of academic expectancy. It wasn't so bad. I regained some of my old friends but more importantly made new ones; among these was Janice.

Janice was my complete opposite, long blonde hair in contrast to my short dark and a figure that was developing curves in all the right places compared to my gangly stick-thin frame, but we clicked. We spent every waking moment together. My confidence grew; I became more assertive, even occasionally answering Dad back. I was 13 and becoming a typical teenage rebel.

I learnt to play this to my advantage. I was growing up, developing. Attending an all-girls school where boys, sex and such like was the main topic of conversation. Lunch hours the stark lack of contents in my lunch bag was easily hidden by incessant chatter of excited voices about the latest pop idol, or hottest boy at the bus stop. I wanted to be part of this so I invented a boyfriend. I based his looks on Barry Sheene the motorbike racer, and his sexual knowledge on embellishment of my past experience.

Uncle Harry's visits became more frequent, two, sometimes three times a week. I knew by now that Mum was having sex with him for money; when he came I would be summoned to go out with Dad for a walk. I began to rebel. Uncle Harry would turn up; on the occasions I opened the door his lustful look as he ran his eyes over my developing body made me shiver with disgust. The day came when enough was enough.

'Hello my lovely.' His smooth sickly voice vomited these hated words into my ears.

'Hello, Uncle Harry.'

I pushed past his small sweaty body to the fresh air outside. What was I to do out there? Dad would be fuming; he would be expecting me to go for a walk with him. I ran as fast as I could towards Janice's house. I stayed there all afternoon. Leaving didn't appeal to me, returning to the anger that was bound to have simmered up to a bubbling fury waiting to erupt in uncontrollable rage; I knew I could expect the worst.

Eventually I returned home; the house was quiet. I knocked. Mum answered.

'Where the hell 'ave you been? Dinner's ready, got your favourite, spaghetti and chop.'

Her smile was genuine. I didn't understand; this was not what I expected at all.

''Ello, pet.'

Dad was nice; what the hell was all this about? In my naivety I decided that I must have taught them a lesson by defiance, but I was so very wrong. They had a plan that was much more to their advantage.

Uncle Harry and his family had a caravan on a holiday site edging the Thames estuary. It was a complete shock when Mum and Dad informed me we were going there for the day. I loved my auntie (Harry's wife) and my cousins were around my age. I was so looking forward to it.

We went; it was heaven. My cousin Sarah and I walked around the site, arms linked, flicking our hair and eying up the boys. I loved the attention.

A few weeks later Mum and Dad asked me if I would like to earn some money cleaning Uncle Harry's caravan. I was elated, money of my own! Saturday morning came, Uncle Harry arrived and I gladly clambered into the car beside him.

'You ready, my lovely?'

'Yep.' I was ready, but not for what he not only expected, but had been promised.

It was a good hour's drive to the caravan; I hated sitting so close to him. I stole a sideways glance at him; I saw his small frame hunched over the steering wheel, his greasy hair parted on the side framing his weak jawline, eyes bright sparkling with unmasked excitement, spittle gathered in shiny drops at the corner of his wet mouth. He turned unexpectedly and caught my gaze. Moving his bony hand to trail his unwelcome fingers across my knee he asked:

'You all right, my lovely?'

I wished he'd stop calling me that. *My name is Anna*, I screamed into the darkness of my repulsed mind.

'Yep.' Thankfully my voice echoed more confidence than I felt.

On arrival we parked outside the caravan, its appeal marred by the grey day that surrounded it. I was nervous; why? We entered the dim interior.

'Where's the cleaning stuff?' I asked as I opened the cupboard under the sink.

'Why?' Uncle questioned me.

I moved to open the curtains to let what little daylight there was join us.

'Don't open them; we don't want everyone seeing in, do we?'

'No, I don't suppose so.' Something wasn't right. A sick feeling bubbled in my stomach, fountaining bile into my throat like some internal natural geyser. I returned my search to the cupboards, distracting my train of thought to the practicalities of what I was there for. I pulled out a washing-up bowl.

'Ahh, there we go, we may need that.' Uncle spoke through yellowing teeth as he twirled a roll-up between his nicotine-stained fingers. His smile widened as his gaze travelled from my feet to meet my eyes. I felt undressed, dirty, scared.

'Let's go to the bedroom first.'

I did as I was told, carrying the empty bowl with me.

'Strip.'

'Uncle, I need to clean your place.' My eyes scurried round the small cubbyhole of a room.

'I don't know why you think you're here, but you're to please me. We wouldn't want to upset your mum and dad, now would we? I don't want to tell them you've been a bad girl. You know what your dad will do to you.'

His words were slow and meaningful, even gentle and caring in a way.

'Now take your clothes off and let me see you.'

I stood awkward, dressed in embarrassment and my knickers. The cool daylight streamed through a gap in the curtains and fell like a pointing finger of guilt across my tiny budding breasts.

'Lovely.' Uncle undid his shirt before releasing the buttons and zip on his trousers. 'You seen one of these before?'

My eyes fell on the area below his waistband where his cock stuck out small and proud. Rapidly I looked away.

'No, no, don't look away.' He grabbed the back of my head, clenching my hair in his fist, forcing my chin to chest. 'You will see lots of these in your life, lots. Think of this as an education, a way of helping you. Take a closer look.'

With his hands on my shoulders he forced me to my knees. Eye to eye with his manhood I shook. The rancid smell of stale sweat and manhood engulfed me, making me gag.

'Don't be scared, it's nice I'm helping you. You'll thank me for this one day. Take a good look.' His hands back in my hair he pulled me forward, closer.

'Kiss it, it won't bite.'

I pulled back hard.

'No, let me go, let me go!' I screamed.

'Stop it, stop!' He pulled me upright, pushing me with force; I lost my balance and fell on the bed.

'I'll tell Dad if you touch me, he'll kill you!'

Uncle Harry sneered, his face mapped with contempt, mirrored in his steely eyes.

'You silly girl, you think your dad doesn't know why I brought you here? Course he does; bloody hell, it's cost me enough.'

I lay still, his words soaking me, the reality drowning me: Dad knows, he sent me here to have sex with Uncle Harry! Does Mum know? Surely not.

Rightly or wrongly I gave in to Uncle Harry's requests. I lay still whilst his fingers explored my nakedness, running over my newly forming breasts, trailing down towards my innocence, removing my knickers and then invading my intimate parts. After a while he mounted me, the heaviness of his body pressing against mine as he fiddled with his semi-hard erection.

'You have to be wet down there for me to get it in. Stop clenching your legs, I only have a little cock, it won't hurt you, I'm breaking you in gently for all the cock you'll have in the future; you'll thank me for this, mark my words.'

Thank him, thank him? I don't think so. The words swam round me, sucking me further and further into the whirlpool of fear and emotion that twisted within me. Although I had resigned myself to my fate my body rebelled; involuntary spasms hardened my thighs against his insistent probing.

'Oh for fuck's sake.' Uncle jumped up, kneeling above me, his semi-hard erection fading fast.

'This is no good, no good at all.' He sat astride me and rested back on his heels.

Elation flooded through me, I had won, I had stopped him. He hadn't, couldn't take me. A deep sigh escaped me as I wriggled beneath him.

'Let me up, let me get up.'

His thoughtful gaze scanned me.

'Not so fast. Just because I can't get my cock in there doesn't mean my money is not well spent. Get up.'

I lay still.

'Get up, stand up, I said.'

I did as I was told, once more standing under the pointy finger of light sifting through the gap in the orange curtains.

'I want a wee.' I knew there was no toilet in the caravan and he would have to let me outside to go to the toilet block. Irrational thoughts raced through my mind. I could run, run

105

away from him, from everyone. I didn't know where, anywhere but here, anywhere but home.

'Piss in the bowl.'

'What?'

'Piss in the bowl.' He rested back on his forearms, splaying his legs wide open.

'Go on, pee in the bowl; you don't think we go to the loos at night, do you? No, we use that.' He nodded towards the bowl sitting in the corner. 'So pee in the bowl.'

'OK.' I resigned myself to my plans being stopped in their tracks, admitting to myself they were unrealistic anyway.

I stood naked; my fingers curled awkwardly round the rim of the orange plastic washing-up bowl, my eyes casting over its emptiness. Thoughts of Uncle Harry standing peeing, his full-force stream of urine splashing noisily, drumming the sides, flitted through my mind. I wanted to vomit.

The pressing urgency to pee was uncomfortable; I knew I couldn't hold on much longer.

'Where shall I go?'

'Pee here, in the bowl, for me. I'm going to watch you.' His hand circled his growing erection; fingers stroked back and forth, rolling the skin up and down. I couldn't help it; it repulsed me yet somehow fascinated me. I watched through dipped lashes as his flesh expanded.

'Put the bowl on the floor, stand astride and pee.'

The bowl fell from my fingers; I squatted, urine readily beginning to descend.

'Stand up.' His voice was stern, angry almost. I did as I was told. Standing astride the bowl, eyes turned to the yellowing ceiling, blinking to fight back the tears of overwhelming humiliation and guilt, I peed for him whilst he played with his erection and brought it to a place of no return. I didn't care if I missed the bowl, pissed on the floor, I just wanted this over. As I finished Uncle stood in front of me, turned me round and sat me on the bed. Eyes level with mine, his throbbing cock grasped by his fast-moving hand, he brought the whole episode to a finale as he exploded sticky fluid over my face and hair.

Alone in the bedroom I dressed, wiping my hair and face on the sheet; I didn't care. Robbed of all dignity and respect I sat on the edge of the bed and waited. Numbness washed over me. The salty smell of sex lingered on my skin; I made the mistake of licking my lips and heaved at the taste.

'You were a good girl; we will have to do things like that more often.'

With one of his hands on the wheel and one on my inner thigh we motored homeward.

I sat silent.

'I'm only helping you, you know. Not all girls get the help I am giving you. You should be grateful. Now don't go telling all your friends because not all mums and dads are as good as yours. They are thinking of your future.'

I still sat in silence, staring through the window of the smoke-filled car watching my life rush by, spiralling out of control, spinning on tilted axis, distorting beyond recognition. Did all parents act like this? Janice had never mentioned it, nor any of my other friends. Perhaps I should keep quiet.

We pulled up outside home; Uncle Harry placed a crumpled £10 note into my hand.

'For you. It's more than I give your mum because you are younger and prettier.'

I took the money; why shouldn't I? That day my child left and a stranger took her place.

The car journey home had been in silence. I thought I should at least be angry or cry, but I wasn't and didn't; instead I was numb, my inner self hushed, dead maybe.

Once we arrived home robotic actions took over. I pushed past Mum when she opened the door. I wanted to say sorry but the word wouldn't come. In the front room

Dad lounged in his chair; there was a strange look on his face, one I hadn't seen before or maybe I had but just hadn't recognised it, a sort of half smile, a smirk. His eyes blazed intense, stripping me naked; was this hate or admiration?

Mum made tea, I sat in silence, Uncle Harry gave Dad money which he quickly gave to Mum and ordered she take to the shops to get him fags.

My new life had begun.

CHAPTER FOURTEEN

The stillness of the cool autumn morning chills the room but I am warm, cosy in my bed, wrapped in the duvet, snuggled into the body-shaped dip that Martin, called into the working day by the intrusive alarm clock, has recently left. I am in a half-doze, content to lie and savour the manly smell of aftershave and body wash that lingers in the room, a reminder of my security. Things could have been so different. In that half place, you know, the one between sleep and consciousness, I find myself thinking about writing this part of this story. Images from way back float in and out of my dream space.

I was 13 or maybe 14 in the same state, lying in bed, my toes reaching the chilled corners. Dawn light filtered through dusty windows; the rattle of milk crates reminded me that shortly Dad would wake and demand his cup of tea. It was nearly 7 am. Whatever day, whatever we were doing, working or not, Dad insisted we all wake up around this time. With nothing to do apart from follow persistent demands and orders the days would always drag.

At 7 am the wind-up clock changed its consistent ticking to a shrill alarming blast, its hammer banging between two brass bells that sat proudly announcing 'WORLD WAKE UP!' and sure enough Mum went clattering into the kitchen to make Dad tea for him to drink in bed. Sitting bolt upright he barked his orders as she scurried around giving him breakfast, fags and morning sex.

I lay with my eyes shut tight savouring the night before. Dad had miraculously allowed me to go with Janice to 'St Peters', the local youth club. Licking my lips I tried to retrieve the taste of Peter and my first ever proper kiss, as a secret smile travelled across my face, unfortunately seen by Dad.

'What you smiling for? Did you get a cock last night?'

Eyes wide open I drank in his stare. Contempt, maybe even hatred in a form, burned inside me; I fought to keep its blaze from igniting my expression, knowing this insolence would gain a response I would sorely regret.

'Yeah, your mother told me you walked out with a boy, she saw you.'

Yes, she had seen me, she had asked, I was excited telling her Peter had asked me out and kissed me good night, she seemed genuinely pleased; so why, why had she told Dad knowing how he would react?

'Your tea's 'ere, leave 'er alone, Dick, come on.'

'I want know if the little bitch got her first taste of cock last night. Well, did you?'

Dad had left his bed; his face was pressed close to mine, his body looming over me. Bolts of fear shot through my body; I expected to cry but I didn't.

'No, no, I didn't get cock,' I screamed uncontrollably. Something had broken; something hidden for many years rose from within and temporarily overtook the fear that was usually my constant companion. Blood pounded in my temples, my heart raced, I had no control over my body or mind as venomous words spewed vile obscenities held onto for so long.

'If I had cock last night it wouldn't be the fucking first time, and you know it.'

Silence hung like a fire blanket, heavy and weighted. I don't think Dad knew quite how to react. The air in the room stilled; all I could hear was my own breathing.

He turned and left the room. I lay stunned not quite knowing what to do.

My drifting dream state is broken by a solitary shaft of sunlight warming my face. Patterns flicker through my closed eyelids as I return to my world.

Whether it was my retaliation or realisation of his own actions Dad backed off. I still got backhanders and filthy looks, there were still arguments but he just seemed... a little wary, even scared of me. It was surreal.

I took advantage of the newfound peace. By now school was far from my priority. The history of absence, lack of friends, bullying mixed with my home-life had changed me. I was removed from the child I once was. I shut my child self in a box and buried her as deep as possible under all the shit that had been piled up over the years. I didn't need her. In her place was a confident, arrogant, sexually aware teenager who fought her corner. Smart, in control (at times anyway) and putting herself first. I suppose in a way I had become a mirror image of Mum and Dad.

CHAPTER FIFTEEN

Combine a mixture of hormones and a lifetime of disjointed events, add a large dollop of physical and mental abuse with a topping of sexual education from a not so well-meaning uncle and by the age of 14, though completely unaware, the real me had taken a back seat and the rebellious, money-orientated, sexually aware go-getter had taken her place.

Like most budding teenage girls my interest in boys was growing. The difference was other girls at school were spending break time talking about their first kiss whereas I sat quietly wondering how much I should give out to gain satisfaction.

It sounds bizarre but I felt in control. I was calling the shots, seeing two, three boys at a time, allowing them more access to my body than they got anywhere else, not letting them go all the way, teasing them to the point where they were panting for me. It will come as no surprise that this made me very popular with the opposite sex in both the youth club and the local town.

At 14 I was still a virgin, or was I? I had not willingly let anyone enter me, in fact didn't remember anyone doing that, but what happened to make me so promiscuous in the first place? Was it just a collection of small incidents throughout my short life or had something more sinister happened that I blocked out or was just too young to recall?

I think back to when just three or four I was pleasuring myself for comfort. I know children do this but do they do it with such determination, such skill or intensity to feel that desired safe emotion? Was I sexually abused to the limit of penetration in infanthood? I will never know.

Janice and I remained firm friends, going to the local youth club two or three times a week, jiving and twirling, shaking our newly formed curves for the benefit of the testosterone-filled youths that edged the dance floor to watch the girls displaying their female form to its best. It's funny but since my outburst Dad didn't seem to mind me going to the youth club; the only thing he insisted on was that Mum walked me the mile or so there and back. Wednesday, Friday and Saturday were my nights. It didn't matter that I wore the same outfit of Mum's brown suede flares and a striped T-shirt; no one cared; it wasn't like it is today when most girls and women hate wearing the same outfit twice on nights out. Clothes were not as plentiful, my wardrobe was scarcer than most... a uniform for school paid for by government grant, two pairs of knickers and two pairs of socks and a scattering of out-of-school clothes that had been handed down from my cousins.

On the nights Janice and I didn't go to St Peters we went into the nearest town, Woolwich. We would sit in the Wimpy bar watching passers-by through the steamy windows, nursing our cup of coffee, sipping it slowly, eking it out as long as possible, waiting for eye candy or in fact any male attention. This is how I met Eddie.

On a cold grey afternoon as we sat cocooned in red plastic bucket seats, noses pressed to the misted windows of Wimpy burger bar, discussing the lack of talent that existed in the boring town of Woolwich, moaning about parents, school and such like, our interest was sparked by a crowd of boys. Quickly leaving the warm café we exited into the chilly late-afternoon air. Following the boys we discussed how the heck we could get their attention because even though we had crossed the road to be opposite them, sped up our pace to be in front of them and put on our best exhibition of bum wiggling they seemed to be oblivious to us.

'Give me a fag.'

'What?' Why did Janice want a fag now of all times? Our concentration shouldn't be on puffing smoke but on not letting the first bit of decent talent we had seen for ages get away.

'One of them is smoking; I'll go ask for a light.'

Janice was always more confident than me. I gave off the air of being self-assured but deep down somewhere a glimmer of my former self, the girl that existed before all the bad stuff took hold, lurked: a shy, quiet, insecure little girl.

'Oi,' Janice yelled at the gang as she crossed the road. They stopped and waited.

A flutter of dark eyelashes against fair skin coupled with long blonde hair and ample busty curves soon had the six or so boys captivated. Janice's infectious bubbly laugh and finely crafted flirting skills did the trick whilst I, lean with olive tanned skin and boyish cropped hair, stood overshadowed by her charm. Don't get me wrong, Janice and I were the very best of friends, we are still in touch to this day; there was no jealousy, just a little envy.

Oh, once in a sexual encounter she was no match for me; she had no idea what my life was like... I never told her or anyone for that matter about any of it. On one hand I was too ashamed, embarrassed; on the other I suppose I thought everyone had much the same life; not the poor parenting or lack of food but the sexual side I imagined was the norm for every teenage girl. One thing I knew for sure: boys seemed more interested in me than her when it came to sex.

'So what's your name?' A tall chubby guy threw the question in my direction.

I found myself staring into deep chocolate-brown eyes that penetrated my very being, falling, falling mesmerised before the shock of capture was shattered by realising that those eyes were framed with the thickest, ugliest glasses I had ever seen, not good for a girl to be seen with.

'Anna.'

'Anna.'

'What?' I asked, sneering at his questioning ignorance.

'Anna. Your name spells the same backwards.'

'Fuck off, thicko,' I replied. His answer was a grin escaping from slightly disarming lips.

I had no time for this; my sights were fixed on the best-looking guy in the group. Janice was already in deep conversation with him but his interest in her didn't bother me; once he knew what I could offer he would drop her as quickly as a hot chip. Friends or not, I had no loyalty. I had to have control of my fate, even if my fate was self-destruction.

The weeks fell into months. I found out the brown-eyed boy was Eddie and the fanciable one was his brother Mick. Eddie continued to chat to me; I continued to ignore him to the point of rudeness.

'I want to ask you a question,' he said one evening.

We were standing under the canopy of Sainsbury's sheltering from the persistent drizzle of a winter's night. I lounged against the handle of an empty shopping trolley as I brooded over the fact that Janice and Mick were now an item.

'What?'

'Will you go out with me?'

'No.'

'Why?'

'Because you're fat and ugly, now piss off and leave me alone.'

The momentary hurt that flickered across that kind unattractive face gave me the briefest pang of guilt before I repaired the crack that dared to flaw my exterior shell. My size six high heel stomped hard on the hidden soul within me, making it cower in fear and retreat back into its hidden depths. I was strong again as I sneered at him.

The question was asked again and again, the answer always the same.

Eddie somehow seemed to win over Mum and Dad. He started coming to our house every night and just sitting and watching TV. I would curl up in the smallest distant corner of my bed and scowl at anyone who dared to look at me. Dad took great delight in this; it was a power trip; he would come out with stupid things like 'You could do far worse than get with this one.' He would nod in Eddie's direction as Eddie offered Dad yet another fag. I don't know who I hated more.

Mum acted weird around Eddie, making him tea, fussing, asking if he was OK, did he want anything. It made me sick; I would often storm out slamming the door behind me, leaving the three of them to their cosy little evening.

Eddie was at our house seven days a week. He worked shifts for British Rail as a signalman so I never knew when he was going to turn up, but regardless I owed him nothing and didn't want to give him anything, especially as Mum and Dad seemed so keen on him. I still gathered as many male admirers as possible and carried on offering more than most girls.

Janice hung around more and more with Mick; they both tried to encourage me to go out with Eddie; I didn't want to know. Though Janice and I remained friends my circle widened as I met others at the youth club; among these were the Smith and Clarke families.

The Smiths and Clarkes were two of the roughest families in Woolwich, but I didn't care between them they had a collection of young kids but more importantly several teenage boys: Ray, Graham, Geoff and a few older whom I don't recall the names of.

Graham was sweet but short and I definitely had a thing for tall dark boys, Ray was an OK looker but a bad boy always in trouble with the police, and Geoff... a 14-year-old girl's dream material... I would have done anything for Geoff, he was my first official crush and the first to break my heart.

Geoff and I had only one real sexual experience. He was a player; at 17 he was a few years older than me, but he still came to the youth club. Gathering in the queue to get in I would position myself ahead of Geoff, knowing that this would give him the best view of my bum and its over-exaggerated wiggle as I climbed the stairs to the beat of Mud, Sweet and Suzi Q beckoning me to the dance floor. Geoff would always comment, 'Nice arse.' I would laugh, before he turned his attention to someone older, leaving me sad... but only for a few minutes; there was always access to a kiss and a grope with someone at St Peters.

The Smiths and the Clarkes lived on the roughest council estate in the area. The families were loud, always in trouble and well known by the law. Despite the many evenings I went to their houses I never met the parents. Maybe the attraction to these boys wasn't just sexual but also that they seemed to have complete control of their own destiny... fucked up thinking, I guess.

One evening at the Smiths' house, when I was snuggled between Geoff and Graham, Geoff put his hand on my knee; his fingers travelled up my thighs and started to caress my crotch. I didn't stop him; why should I? What happened next felt weird; he took my hand and led me to the bedroom. As we went toward the stairs Geoff beckoned to Graham to follow us. I lay on the bed and let those boys do whatever they wanted, stopping just short of intercourse. It was the first time I tasted a man's cock willingly. They both wanked over me, coming simultaneously. I remember all I was concerned about was getting spunk on my T-shirt.

It was getting boring, going out almost every night, meeting the same boys, giving the same sexual favours. Dad had started to harden again, stopping me going out, telling me not to be so rude and to stay in with Eddie. *Fuck Eddie*, I thought.

On one such night when I was kept in I sat and brooded. Mum and Dad sat on the two armchairs pushed against the side of their bed, which left me no choice but to sit next to Eddie on my bed.

'A fine night, fucking weirdo family all huddled in the front room, if that's what you can call it.' My mumbling caught Eddie's ears. He just shot me a look and said nothing. I grumbled on.

I was so bored; how could I spice up the evening? And then an idea started to form in my fucked-up head. I shuffled nearer to Eddie, giving him an encouraging smile. His brow crinkled with confusion. I moved closer; with little discreet movements eventually my legs lay stretched out against his. He did what many boys did when they wanted to get close. Scared of rejection, rather than make a positive move he stretched his arms above his head, casually letting one drop over my shoulders. I didn't move. I could feel his racing heartbeat against me. We sat for what seemed an era; I saw Dad glance over and nudge Mum, nodding towards us to show his approval. It wasn't his approval I was interested in. It wasn't Eddie I was interested in; I just wanted to spice up my evening, a sort of payback time to Dad, showing him that his control had no effect on me.

Sliding into a closer position I removed Eddie's arm from my shoulders and placed his hand on my thigh, all the time watching Dad's reaction. Dad looked straight ahead at the telly but I am sure that he caught glimpses of what I was doing from the corner of his eye.

'I'm going to get into my nightie.' I said it out loud to no one in particular.

My nightie was short; like the majority of my clothes it was ill-fitting, too small, but on this occasion it was just right for what I wanted.

I slid myself back onto the bed next to Eddie and pulled the counterpane over my lap and legs. Grabbing his hand I slid it under the cover to touch my thigh. He said nothing, but kneaded my bare skin with his soft large hands. I was quite nice and even nicer when his hand slid further up and his fingers stroked the gusset of my knickers. I let him slip one finger inside me; he still kept his eyes fixed front and didn't say a word. Mum and Dad were oblivious to what we were doing; the thrill it gave me was unimaginable. I was in control.

Later that night when Eddie left I showed him to the door. He kissed me, I let him. Much to my disgust I enjoyed his soft lips on mine.

The next day I had to make sure things returned to normal. No one could know about what happened between me and Eddie, I didn't want to be associated with him, I definitely didn't fancy him... did I?

CHAPTER SIXTEEN

Love and sex, two things I confused for a large part of my life. According to research it is common. From my perspective I felt that if someone, no matter who, wanted me, then surely they must love me? It stems, as do all of our traits and emotional education, from childhood. When I was a young child Dad wanted me to sit on his lap; he showed me attention, his loving arms wrapped round me. I now know that at times the reason was for his personal gratification, he used me to obtain self-pleasure, but as a child the emotional behaviour was already carving the grooves and laying the tracks of the tune titled '*Sex and love are one and the same*'. Wrong, but it took years to find out. I didn't start to accept or even realise that another human being could love me for what and who I am and not for what I could give them until I met my husband. I was 28; even then it took years of his unconditional love, many mistakes on my part and his, fierce rows and even a short separation for me to finally come to the place where I am now and our marriage to flourish.

Twenty-eight years is a long time to fill a suitcase with fucked-up emotional baggage, but my husband has painstakingly supported me and encouraged me to empty this suitcase. It is thanks to him and a few very good friends and counsellors that I have re-packed neatly and though I will never be able to rid myself of the memories and scars of the past, the suitcase is within the weight limit and rarely robs me of the precious moments in my life. But that wasn't the case at the age of 15.

Uncle Harry was still visiting; I avoided him at all cost. Whenever he arrived his smarmy look would sweep over me, drinking in every line; I knew he was thinking of the caravan event and how long it would be before he could get me there again. Mum and Dad had tried to persuade me on more than one occasion, oh yes, the usual bullshit about going to clean the caravan… As a rebellious 15-year-old I knew it was bollocks and all they wanted was to farm me out for Uncle Harry's pleasure and reap the financial benefits.

Dad resigned himself to the fact that I would disappear out on my own whenever Uncle Harry turned up. Dad stayed in. On the one occasion I returned home whilst Uncle Harry was still there, I found Dad standing in the kitchen smoking a fag and sipping a mug of tea. Mum and Uncle were in the front room; according to Dad they were measuring up for a wardrobe… ha ha ha. Now it is laughable, the pathetic pretence that they tried to portray to stop me realising Mum was having sex for money. What they either didn't or pretended not to realise was that I had drawn the obvious conclusion many years before but I had never discussed it with anyone.

Kenneth was still sniffing round Mum as well. He would turn up, sometimes when Dad was out, but that was a very rare occurrence because as usual Dad was once again unemployed. I already knew from what I had seen at the age of ten that Mum was having an affair with Kenneth; what I couldn't make out was whether Dad knew they were sleeping together. One minute Dad would encourage this man round and even let Mum go for a drink with him, the next he would be raging and screaming and accusing them of having an affair. He even went as far as ringing Kenneth's company and telling them he was coming to ours in work time, hoping Kenneth would get sacked. Some days if Kenneth came round when Dad was out, on his return Dad would inspect the bed, sniffing the bedding and checking for indents shaped like heads or bodies. I used to think Dad was wrong to do this, but really was he? The evidence was all there. It would have been so easy for me to open my mouth and confirm his suspicions but I didn't. I felt sorry for Mum and what he put her through, the bullying, the control, the mental putting down, but then again I felt sorry for Dad. I was truly stuck in the middle, and torn apart.

Kenneth still scared me. He was in the fire that killed my brother; he had lived in the flat above ours, the attic flat. Asbestos was widely used as a fire retardant in the sixties so when the house was converted into flats it was used between the floors as a barrier. When the fire did break out the asbestos worked, the flames were contained in our flat but the asbestos heated up to impossible temperatures. Whilst trying to save his wife and children Kenneth was overcome by heat and lay unconscious on the floor until rescued by the fire department. Due to this he was in a special burns unit for a very long time: in excess of a year, I believe. His body sustained over 50% burns and he had a mass of skin grafts, therefore was and always will be covered in scars. Before collapsing Kenneth managed to save his three young sons but as I have mentioned before his wife fell from the roof and broke her neck, consequently she died instantly.

Another day much as many others, empty stomach, no food, no money; with Dad having no fags he was unbearable. I received so many slaps that day that I lost count, slap for insolence, slap for being noisy, slap for sitting wrong, slap for breathing... you get the picture.

There was a little reprieve from the situation when Kenneth arrived. I sat huddled in the corner of my bed hugging my knees as he came into the room. He was always polite to me but the sight of him just repelled me; all he got from me was a grunt in return.

Mum told him she couldn't make him a drink as we had no milk or money to get any. She went on to explain that Big Nan could lend her £5 but she didn't have the bus fare to get there to get the money in the first place. I think Mum was hoping he would offer either a lift or money. She was right, he offered a lift.

'I have my car today; do you want me to take you over there?' His eyes sparkled with hidden agenda.

'Oh yes, thanks.' Mum's breathless answer left nothing to the imagination and Dad picked up on this.

'We got stuff to do 'ere, she can go with 'im.' Dad nodded in my direction.

'Yes, I'll go,' I eagerly replied; an opportunity to escape the suffocating environment and see Big Nan as well; excellent. Kenneth hesitated.

'Fine,' he said, unenthusiastically.

Mum's fury seeped from every pore of her body. Blood rushed to her cheeks; her skin glowed a fiery red.

'Anna doesn't want to go, I'll go. She can stay 'ere with you.'

'No, no, I don't mind.' I rushed to stop Dad changing his mind. The chance to get out, I wasn't going to let that escape me. OK, yes, the man creeped me out a little but over the years I suppose he had proved harmless; he was just weird to look at.

Mum seethed. Her gaze held mine. I had never seen her act like this. She stormed from the room slamming the door behind her.

'What's her problem?' No one answered me but I knew Dad would lose his temper with her the minute we were gone.

I climbed into the passenger seat of the 1970s Citroën. Kenneth climbed in beside me and started the engine. For the first mile or two we drove in silence.

'So, how are you getting on at school then?' he eventually asked.

'OK.' I squeezed my reply through unresponsive lips.

'No boyfriend yet?'

None of your fucking business, I wanted to say. 'Loads, thanks,' I answered.

A pensive silence followed; the atmosphere seemed to change as the miles went by.

'You know I was in the fire.'

Of course I fucking know, I thought. The unspoken words sat amid my breath held in silence.

'I was very ill, you know.'

I wriggled uncomfortably against the vinyl seat. I don't know why but something made me wary; all my senses were alert. My heart raced in my chest, its beat resounding so hard that it echoed in my throat. I felt sick.

'Of course your mum has helped me out, helped me to get better, you know.'

His voice was soft, running over me like treacle, thick and sweet; I had heard this tone before. My breathing shallowed.

Kenneth pulled his car into a layby on Shooters Hill, a few miles short of Big Nan's house. He turned toward me, swinging his legs around until his knees were within touching distance of mine. He reached over with his scarred wrinkled hand and touched my bare leg, stroking his finger from naked knee to skirt hem.

'I was on tablets for a long time to make this work.' He placed his other hand on his crotch and squeezed himself.

'Your mum made sure I knew they were working, but now the doctors have stopped them, to see if I'm better down there.' He nodded his head towards the hand that now massaged his hardening cock.

I was frozen, unable to speak or move. What was it with men? I wanted to vomit. His hand still worked my leg, travelling further under my skirt each time.

'So are you going to help me? I'll make it worth your while.'

He was leaning so close that I could smell the full stench of the Capstan Full Strength on his breath filling my nostrils.

'I don't do things like that.'

'Oh come on, it will be fun, all you have to do is give this a little rub.'

Without me even realising it he had unzipped his trousers and had his cock in his hand. I couldn't help but glance down; morbid curiosity consumed me. Was his cock the same as Uncle Harry's? Was it scarred and wrinkly? All I saw was the head of his penis peeking through the top of his clenched hand as it moved up and down.

'Either let me out the fucking car or take me to my nan's. I don't care which, but if you don't put that pathetic thing away and drive not only will I tell Mum that her boyfriend tried to fuck me, but I will tell Dad about you and Mum.' The strength I displayed on the surface wasn't mirrored inside.

He pulled the car into the flow of traffic. The rest of the journey was travelled in silence. As we pulled up outside home he turned to me and said, 'Don't tell your mum, will you?'

I sneered and got out of the car, slamming the door behind me.

Once I had given the money I got from Big Nan to Mum, both she and Dad went out. Silence fell on our empty flat. The enormity of what had happened in the car engulfed me. Was it me? Did I just look like an easy lay? It must be my fault... It must be me... First the possible sexual abuse as a young child, then the way Dad used to wriggle me on his lap, the man who touched me when I was playing at the end

125

of Brent Road, Uncle Harry at the caravan and now this. It was me. I was convinced it was me, though what I did to make these men do these despicable things to me, I had no idea.

I remember thinking, *At least now I am in control. I say when and where a boy can touch me. It is my choice. At least I give to who I want, and they come back for more. I must be good.* This thought used to thrill me during times of sexual activity as well as when I pleasured myself for comfort in the lonely hours.

By the time I was 15 we had moved again, this time not too far so I managed to stay at the same school. Because of the amount of time I was absent the school appointed me a welfare officer named Mrs Barley. I saw her every week in school in a little office off the main hall. There she would ask me questions and I would give the answers that kept her off my back. She would sit in a swivel chair and smoke a cigar. The weeks that I was not so forthcoming with talking, she would offer me a puff of her cigar, which I greedily took; it made me feel special... just as the sexual attention from all the boys and a few girls did.

Eddie and I carried on petting. Boys came and went but I couldn't help always falling back on a bit of fun with Eddie. Again I thought this was control, but actually in all honesty, though I would have rather died than admitted it, I quite enjoyed the things he did to me.

I had got bored with St Peters and taken to hanging around with Janice and the crowd again. Most of the boys now had motorbikes and one or two had cars.

At the end of the evenings we spent together trawling the streets of Woolwich we would split; Eddie, Janice and I would get a lift in Mick's car. Often Janice would have to be home before me. Dad liked Eddie and Mum still fussed and swooned over him, so there was never a problem about me going out with him; they both positively encouraged it.

126

Dad I am sure did this because Eddie often brought him fags and gave him money… Dad knew when he was on to a good thing, but then again Eddie was just buying them to get to me.

Janice and Mick had gone all the way; she thought he was the one. Mick was about to join the army and be posted initially to Taunton for training and then on to more foreign lands once he had his passing out parade. Janice had given in to full sex, wanting to keep him interested. She thought they were in love. It made me nauseous the way they both carried on… I was jealous, she had it all, love, affection, attention and sex; I wanted it.

On the way home Eddie and Mick sat in the front of the car; Mick was proud of his Ford Escort Popular Plus and rattled on about its performance whilst Janice and I sang the latest chart hits from our back seat position. Janice was dropped home first. Her loving but fairly strict Catholic upbringing meant she had to be in by nine whereas I had till 10.30.

'Let's go for a drive, it's still early,' Eddie suggested as we left Janice.

'OK.' I was happy; the longer I could avoid going home, the better.

We ended up at Chislehurst Common. Silhouettes of branches backlit by the moonlight reached toward the car; frankly I was scared. I had been scared of the dark ever since the fire.

'I'm getting out for a fag,' Eddie announced. 'Coming?'

'Not fucking likely,' I replied.

'You can sit in the front for a bit if you like, whilst I'm gone.'

I scrabbled from the rear cramped position and slid into the seat already warmed from Eddie's presence, grateful for the luxury of stretching away my stiffness. Mick and I sat in silence. He stretched and dropped his arm over the back of my seat.

'I like you, you know.'

My heart raced; I still fancied him, and I always had since the night we had all met.

He leant over to kiss me; I let him. Let him? Wrong statement; I practically jumped on him. Within seconds his hands were all over me. I never gave Eddie a second thought.

Mick pushed it. Contrary to how free with sexual favours I was I had still never willingly had intercourse so classed myself as a virgin.

Mick eagerly touched every part I would allow him. I had waited so long for this so there were very few holds barred. Before long he was kneeling in the front footwell, his erect penis banging hard against the damp exterior of my knickers... I wanted it yet still fear gripped me, images of Uncle Harry's sweaty manhood flashed a slideshow through my mind, pictures of Kenneth's wrinkled brown burnt skin brushing against my innocence rattled my stomach to a nauseous state.

'No, Mick.' I pushed hard against his shoulders. 'No. I can't.'

His disappointment showed even in the darkened car.

'OK, OK.' He held his hands up to reassure me. He must have heard the swell of panic in my voice.

He kissed me again, whispering, trying to tease and coax me. I allowed his fingers to find my moisture, lying back to enjoy the pleasurable sensation that swept over me. I was back in control. A few more minutes of heavy petting and Mick said he wanted a fag so got out of the car. Eddie slipped into the driver's seat.

'All right?'

'Yeah.' The heat I had so recently felt between my legs now raged in my cheeks. Had he seen us and what we were doing?

Eddie leant towards me, placing his hand on my thigh.

'Fuck off.' I pushed him roughly away.

'You didn't mind Mick doing it; I thought he would have warmed you up for me.'

A feeling of utter despair and emptiness washed over me, a tsunami of emotion threatening to drown my sanity; I swam for the shore of reason, fighting against the current. The waves of echoing words shouted against flood defences, crashing down walls I had so carefully built over the year. I was no better than Mum, no better, I was a whore like her.

'Take me home,' I whispered through my tears.

In my bed that night I lay listening to Dad's snoring. A reassuring sound; where there was breath there was life. I concentrated on the regularity of my own breathing, in, out, in, out… I had life, my life. I didn't want to be like them, not like Mum and Dad; I wanted more.

CHAPTER SEVENTEEN

Love is a fragile entity. We search sometimes unknowingly for love, seeking it out. Love is the staple diet of our emotional side and our soul. I have never made a conscious decision to look for love, but that night I lay in my bed and listened to Dad breathing I did make the conscious decision to be in charge of my own destiny.

The morning dawned misty but with the promise of a warm day hanging on the horizon. I woke early, washed, dressed and went for a walk. My footsteps fell on dirty pavements lined with rows of identical flats, most of which still had the curtains shut tight. A child's cry pierced the otherwise quiet streets. For a second I froze; was he or she OK? Fear ran over me; like a lorry driving over cobbles I shook and grumbled, before completing my journey back home.

I opened the door, letting the smell of cleanliness wash over me. Our home always smelt of polish or disinfectant, sterile, but I knew different; all the cleaning products in the world couldn't clean away the filth swept under our rug, sins hidden but not forgotten.

Dad was up, and Mum; I had been longer than I thought.

'You been out all night?'

I didn't want to rise to the bait.

'No, Dad, just I have been for a walk.' My voice came out as submissive as I could possibly make it.

'Fucking liar, you're a whore, been whoring 'ave you, like your mother; dirty pair of bitches.'

Before I got time to defend myself or Mum a shower of scalding tea rained down over me. Dad had stood up and thrown his tea at me. I sat dripping. The redness of my face was a mixture of anger, hatred and heat from the tea. Salt mixed with sweetness as tears added to the sticky mess I now was.

'Go get a fucking wash, you dirty whore.'

I did just that.

As the tepid water splashed against the white porcelain I let my tears run freely. Why? Why did Dad hate me so much? I had to get out of this, out of here. A plan of action began to hatch.

A few days later I landed a job at a florist; the money wasn't much, £12.50 a week, of which I had to give Mum and Dad £10.

Eddie was still visiting regularly. I coveted his attention, returned his eager fumbling and encouraged his kisses. I can't say I was falling in love but I did care for him. His stable solid persistence and laid-back personality were a refreshing change from the verbal beating down I was used to. Mum and Dad were over the moon. I cottoned on; the more time I spent with Eddie, the more lenient they became.

Eddie was promoted to a railway signalman, taking charge with others at Charlton signal box; he worked shifts including nights. Occasionally I would go to work with him, sitting sipping tea in a box high on stilts, listening to the ding-ding alarm to alert us of an approaching train, when levers would need to be pushed and switches tripped to allow the thundering carriages along their way.

It was in that signal box where I willingly lost my virginity. It was the day after my sixteenth birthday. Eddie had spoilt me, buying me six-inch heeled platform boots and a tight-fitting catsuit in blue denim. (Remember this was the seventies.) He was on night shift and I was with him. We talked a lot in that signal box. I told him some, but not all of what I had endured; he filled in a lot of the blanks for himself. Conversation runs easy at 2 am when the world is sleeping and your defences are down. Eddie confessed that at the age of 14 he was seduced by his aunt 15 years his senior; she had continued to assist with his sexual education for a further two years. He said when he had met me he had realised he wanted more; he said he fell in love the first time he saw me and knew he wanted to marry me. I baulked at the thought yet couldn't explain the warm flow that ran through my veins at the words he uttered. We kissed; he held me for what seemed an eternity. Without even thinking about how or why we ended up touching each other as we had many times before. I closed my eyes and enjoyed the freedom of not having to squirm discreetly under the scrutiny of Dad's watchful eyes. Opening my legs I let his fingers explore my most intimate parts before his tongue took over.

I gasped for his touch, longed for more. Found myself lost in sensations I had never felt. Eddie with his pre-learnt expertise worked my body into a position where I was on all fours, elbows resting on the hard bench, face pressed close to the window staring into the night sky, and there he took me, entering me with slow persuasion. At first I hated it, the hard flesh filling me, but as he moved from a slow to a faster, more determined pace I opened like a flower to the sun, greedily drinking him in, moving with the rhythm he set. He exploded into me, I panicked, no protection, but the thought was dismissed in an instant.

'Marry me.'

'What?'

'Marry me,' he repeated. And there in the afterglow I returned the answer he had waited so long to hear.

The fact we had used no protection returned to nag at me over the next few days until eventually my welcomed period arrived and I could breathe a sigh of relief.

The following few weeks went in a blur. Eddie couldn't wait to tell Mum and Dad and all our mates. I went with the flow, but in the time I was alone my calculated thoughts knew it was so wrong yet so right to become Mrs Maynard. Eddie's parents were devastated; they wanted so much more for their son. His dad worked in parliament; they had a nice house in the suburbs. They saw me as a low-class girl from an even lower-class family. They were right. Because of their distaste Eddie spent all his free time at our house. Dad stopped the pretence, even he couldn't hold a front for the amount of time Eddie was around, and before long Eddie saw the full force of my life with its arguments, beatings and mental anguish. Out of respect he never stepped in, but more and more we would go out or stay at a friend's house.

One day I returned home and Eddie went off to work. I said my goodbyes with a long dutiful kiss and closed the door, heavy hearted that I now had to endure a whole day at home.

'Glad you're 'ome; we've arranged a photographer to take your picture.'

'What?' My spine prickled with awareness. 'What sort of picture?' But Dad was at ease, smiling, in good form, so I let my defences slip.

'You'll be a married woman soon, but you're still our little girl, so we wanna picture of you before you go and get all grown up, don't we Barb?'

'Yeah, yeah we do.' Mum smiled and nodded in agreement.

'OK.' Still slightly wary, I agreed.

'Go get ready then, 'e'll be 'ere soon; you wanna look your best, don't you?'

I nodded in agreement and went to my room.

I chose a brown zip front velour cardigan, jeans and a T-shirt before returning to the front room for Dad's approval.

'No, no, that's no good,' he exclaimed as I stood in front of him. 'Get a skirt on. Make yourself look like the girl you are.' I removed myself from his view, leaving him with his mumblings.

A few minutes later I returned and stood in the doorway.

'Will this do?' I enquired.

His eyes strayed from the TV to loom in my direction.

'Come 'ere, come 'ere in front of me.'

I moved to where he gestured. Dad pulled me toward him, his hands on either side of my hips. His eyes roved from my chestnut-coloured freshly brushed shoulder-length hair down to my zipped cardigan, which I hadn't changed. The fingers of his left hand fumbled with the zip fob, pulling it down to reveal more of my blossoming cleavage; I had chosen to remove the T-shirt underneath. My slender frame shuddered either from the touch or the thoughts I could read mirrored in his dirty perverted mind. With a swift glance he took in the rest of my appearance, shortish cord skirt and my newly acquired platform boots before nodding his approval that coincided with the rap of the knocker.

Duke was a swarthy man, suited, wearing a shirt a little too big round the neck and a tie pulled a little too tight for his collar. He rubbed his finger round inside the ring of material that obviously irritated his neck, leaving a grimy stain, a mixture of sweat and dirt from his damp hands. His smile made me uneasy. His eyes fixed on mine as he clicked together the selected lenses for the job.

'Right, where are we going then?' His question was directed at Dad, not me. I stood awkward, waiting for direction.

'Go in 'er room.'

'Why?' My kneejerk reaction was sharp and sudden, piercing the air with an unnaturally shrill tone. Dad stared fixedly at me; the coldness radiated from his frozen smile.

'Better light.' His softened smile wasn't mirrored in his still icy eyes.

'Lead the way.' Duke gestured, waving his arm across his expanded midriff and bowing slightly.

My feet dragged heavily, pushed forward by Dad's stare.

Once in the bedroom Duke directed me, asking me to stand by the window, smile, not smile, look up, turn sideways; as the orders went on I relaxed, quite enjoying my time in front of the camera.

'Now sit on your bed.' I did willingly.

He leant toward me, shoving the lens close to my face; my laughter became a self-conscious giggle. When he dropped the camera from his face it dangled as a heavy weight at his side. With his free hand he reached for my cardigan zip.

'Let's drop this, shall we?'

My hand shot up in defence.

'Now now, relax, you're beautiful. You could make a lot of money if you just showed a little willing.'

I moved to stop him again; rising from the bed I hissed, 'Fuck off, pervert, or I'll tell my dad.'

Rather than step back as I expected he shoved me down forcing me to sit. His hands dug in to my shoulders as he leant forward and whispered.

'You think your dad doesn't know? I don't pay good money for fucking portrait shots. Now do as you're fucking told or I'll tell your dad and believe me he won't be happy at having to return the £20 I gave him.'

It took a few moments to swallow the sickening pill I had just been prescribed, but as I digested each word I knew he was telling the truth. I sat still as he undid my top and pulled at my nipples to perk them up for the shot. I was allowed to keep my skirt on but had to remove my knickers and put a long hard object into my vagina; probably a dildo, I'm not sure. I was on autopilot. It was the most humiliating experience to date in my entire life. The camera clicked and clicked as I obeyed powerless. It still scares me to think I don't know what happened to those photos.

The date for our engagement was set for Christmas 1976. The party was to be held at Eddie's parents' house. They

135

did not approve but knew that Eddie and I were determined so they did as much as they could by taking control of the situation and arranging everything to limit damage to their reputation. It was blatantly clear that we were of the wrong class when my parents were not included on the small selective guest list cut to a minimum by Eddie's mum.

A few weeks before Christmas my cousin Kerry left her wife-beating, drunken husband for the final time and Dad, seeing this as extra income, invited her and her young daughter to come and stay with us. I couldn't stand the hypocrisy of Dad droning on about how a man should look after his wife and respect his family and she was best off without such a bastard. Eddie and I took to sitting in my bedroom.

One night just before our impending engagement party Eddie and I lay snuggled on my bed. He had been withdrawn, quiet as if something weighed heavy on his mind.

'What's wrong?' I asked for the umpteenth time. He was silent. I rested up on my elbow and looked into his liquid brown eyes. Did I love this man? I wondered. How could I know? I had no concept of love; it was an emotion that remained twisted and marred within the depths of my damaged make-up.

Eddie got up. I watched concerned as this man I cared for paced the room in anguish.

'Is it the engagement? Do you still want to marry me?' I was hesitant, scared of the answer being no but just as scared of it being yes.

He stood as far away from me as the room would allow.

'I need to tell you something.'

The suffocating silence hung only broken by the distant drone of the TV filtering from the room next door.

'What? What is it?' I could hear a heartbeat; was it mine or his?

'I've had sex with someone else.'

Time hung suspended in a frozen moment before the words melted into me; cold drips of reality trickled into my receptive mind. I was not expecting this, not from the ever faithful Eddie.

'Who?'

'It doesn't matter.'

'Yes, yes it does.'

The heartbeat sound grew louder, echoing, momentarily distracting me from the news I had just heard.

'I can hear my heartbeat,' I said.

'No, it's mine. It does that sometimes, makes a funny noise.'

'Who?' I repeated, ignoring what he had just said. 'Is it someone I know?' My voice came across calm and directive, contrary to the fact that it had ridden on a retch.

His hesitation answered my question.

'Is it Janice?'

He looked incredulously at me. 'Fuck no, get a grip, she's my brother's girlfriend.'

'Fiancée,' I corrected.

'Whatever,' he mumbled. 'No, it's not her.'

'Then who?' I reeled off a string of people it might be without giving him time to respond, each name igniting my anger to a fevered pitch.

'Kerry?'

'No, give me credit; your cousin is not exactly the hottest, is she?'

He had a point; since my cousin Kerry had come to stay with us she had spent most of her time in a dirt-stained dressing gown, mooching around carrying her greasy hair and grubby screaming daughter.

'WHO?' I had run out of options as to who the hell it could be.

The silence returned to hang, suffocating any further words but his admission as to who it was.

'Your mum.'

137

I wanted to stand, to hit him, to scream, to be sick but I was paralysed. The heartbeat sound gathered pace, emitting a hissing echo. Time stood still, then slowly but surely everything started to move in slow motion.

I heard my words before I felt them. 'Get out; go home; get away from me.' My voice was alien to me; it sounded like a stranger yelling in the room.

Eddie rushed to my side, fell on his knees and begged me to forgive him. I think he said he was sorry; it had just happened; he felt sorry for her. I didn't want the details.

'Please don't tell her I told you, don't tell your dad. It was a mistake, a stupid, stupid mistake.'

'Get out.'

He left firing a begging shot in my direction but it bounced off my bulletproof being, just leaving yet another scar to join the rest.

I sat for ages locked in a prison of silence that had shock for walls and disgust for a door. The padlock was clenched with a chain of hatred. Eventually it was a gentle knock on my door that released me.

'You OK, love?' Kerry's subdued voice told me that she had heard my sobbing. I hadn't even known the tears were there but now the soaked pillow stuck to my face and web of matted damp hair splayed at all angles told me I had been crying for a long while.

I sat up. 'Yes, fine, just a tiff.' I couldn't tell her, tell anyone about the disgusting betrayal of my mother and my future husband. How could his hands have been on her? How could she have let him? Was it her or him that made the move first? It was obvious from what Eddie had said, begging for me not to tell Dad, that this hadn't been one of Mum's usual sexual favours for a fiver, so it must have been real desire, real sex, not a commodity or means to an end.

I vomited, there and then on the floor beside my bed. Kerry sat beside me until the last of the heaving left my shocked shattered body.

'I'll make you a cuppa.'

I replied with a silent nod.

Later that evening I went to the front room.

'If you're fucking ill piss off to your room, I don't wanna catch it.'

'I'm not ill, I'm just upset.'

'Yeah, so we heard, see he's left you then. What did you do, fuck someone else? Poor bloke, he's a good 'un he is, poor bastard getting mixed up with someone like you. Still he's worth a bob or two. If I were you I'd go grovel for forgiveness, you cheap little slut.'

'I haven't done anything wrong.' My bitter tone was directed at Dad but my eyes were fixed on Mum. She held my stare and although she shifted uncomfortably in her seat a small smile danced on her thin lips. She knew, she knew all right, but I would bide my time before giving her the satisfaction of wallowing in her triumph.

Eddie spent weeks begging. Dad used our break-up as an excuse to move, saying I was broken-hearted and he felt so sorry for me he wanted to give me a fresh start. I just followed choiceless.

CHAPTER EIGHTEEN

There are different sides to each and every one of us. We all have weaknesses and strengths. In different circumstances we adapt our strengths to suit. But what if your weakness is a flaw in your personality? That is how I see the arrogant hard-nosed individual I had become in my teens. The actions that followed Eddie's infidelity were out of my control and not just because I was a stroppy hormone-filled 16-year-old. Acts of self-preservation are sometimes seen not for what they are but for what they portray on the surface, but look deeper and quite often you will discover hurt, anguish and lack of self-esteem under the hard scabbed surface that hides a map of emotional scars.

The move from London to the countryside surroundings of the outskirts of Sevenoaks in Kent was as uneventful as all the rest. Dad had a job on a fruit farm, which as usual came with accommodation. The farm cottage semi set on a hillside with sweeping views over acres of orchards and farmland did nothing to lighten my mood.

Since Eddie and I had broken up his persistent requests for my forgiveness had dwindled. I missed him and the crowd of friends that were now so many miles away.

Mum and Dad never asked why we had cancelled the engagement but I knew Mum had a good idea.

I landed a job in an industrial laundry in the local village of Seal. It meant a two-mile walk each way. To get to work by 7 am I had to leave home at six. It was a dark and lonely walk down a country lane cloaked with many trees and few houses. To say I was nervous would be an understatement, but it was a means to an end. Out of my £15 wages I gave £12 board to my parents and lent them the best part of the rest over the course of the week leading up to payday. Of course I rarely if ever got the money back. Saving for my release from my 16 years of hell was a long slow process.

One day in my lunch hour I went to the village hairdressers. It was payday and I had just about had enough of giving up hard-earned cash. I knew it would cause hell when I got home but I was adamant, for once I was going to do something for me and have my hair done. It was there I met Jenny, a vibrant woman, a few years older than me. We fast fell into a friendship. Jenny lived a few miles past my house so most nights she would take me pillion on her Vespa and drop me home. Dad hated it, calling me a lesbian and banning me from seeing her. I ignored him.

One evening we pulled up and hopped off the Vespa; after giving Jenny a quick hug I ran up the steps to our house. Dad opened the door. There was nothing unusual about that as he hardly bothered with work nowadays; basically we were sitting waiting to be evicted once again.

'What do you want?'

'What?' I didn't understand.

'Go on, fuck off with your lesbo friend, we don't want you here.'

'Dad, don't be stupid, it's dark and cold, let me in.' I went to go up the final step.

'I said fuck off.' His words came with venomous force but not as much force as he used to push me backwards down the stone steps. Tumbling out of control I landed on the hard ground. By the time my body stilled the front door was shut, but the shouting battled within. The words were indistinct as I just lay there soaking in what just happened but I did hear Mum crying and shouting for him to let me in.

Standing I tried to examine my knee through the rip in my trousers, but the dark made it impossible to see; all I could do was feel the sticky warm ooze of blood-soaked cloth against torn scraped skin. I winced with pain. I knocked but there was no way I was getting in. So I started the long walk along the dark country lane towards Jenny's house. I wasn't sure where it was, I had never been there but she had told me her address. Sharp shallow breaths mixed with salty tears accompanied me all the way. Some hours later I stumbled through Jenny's front door in a complete mess. It took time for me to sob the story. Short spurts blurted tormented words. Swollen eyes screwed tight did nothing to block out the imagined and witnessed images that flashed through my mind as I spilled out the agony of the past few years.

She listened, sometimes tight-lipped; sometimes I saw the flash of anger in her eyes and her mouth silently formed the word '*bastard*'.

Despite how I felt I slept, spent of all strength and emotion; I had bared myself for the first time. I was exhausted.

The next day was Friday; we were woken by a loud knocking. Jenny opened the door and escorted two policemen into the room.

'Anna Carter?'

'Yes,' I replied; what the hell did they want?

'Come on, love, you need to come with us.'

'Why?'

'Your parents are worried about you, you didn't tell them where you were or that you would be staying out all night.'

I opened and shut my mouth like a goldfish gasping for air. This was ridiculous!

'No!' I tried to explain what had happened but I could see in their faces that Dad had spun such a good tale that they didn't believe a word I said. As I got ready I listened to them cautioning Jenny about harbouring a minor, explaining that without my parents' permission I was under their control until I was 18.

Returning home was my only choice. I stood humiliated whilst Dad thanked the officers and they lectured me about respect and how lucky I was to have good parents; huh, if only they knew, if only they listened.

I spent the day in my room; there was no food offered to me. Mid-afternoon Mum came up and reminded me it was Friday and I had better go to work and get my wages. As I left a parting shot from Dad fired past me.

'Tell them you were sick today, not that you were with your lesbian lover all night, filthy whore.'

I returned home, gave them the money, went to my room, waited until Dad had done his ten o'clock ritual and the house was quiet. I slipped down the stairs, through the front door and out into the stillness of the night. Once cloaked by the safety of darkness I followed the hedgerows to Jenny's.

On my arrival Jenny was delighted to see me. 'Come in, we're having a party.'

The room throbbed with bass and pulsating bodies. I knew no one but before long I was in the thick of it throwing the newfound delights of vodka and orange down my throat.

Stepping over fallen bodies crashed, I asked Jenny where I should sleep.

'Come share with me.' She took my hand as we giggled our way to her room, like schoolgirls bunking off; we escaped the last few stray individuals still standing among the collapsed bodies that covered the front room floor.

Jenny was quick to strip to her underwear and jump between the sheets. I hesitated unsure.

'Oh come on, get in, for fuck's sake; it's cold out there.' She threw back the blankets and patted the bed.

I grinned; 'OK,' I agreed, shedding my clothes and climbing in beside her.

'Night, chick,' she said as she planted a kiss on my cheek.

'Night,' I replied, turning away from her. Moments later she snuggled in to spoon me. I lay still, rigid, holding my breath not because I was scared, because it was nice as her warm body wrapped into mine. I felt safe. I lay in the darkness and wondered if Dad was right; was I a lesbian? The thought didn't last because moments later the warm currents of sleep overcame me.

The weekend ended with a rude awakening, police at the door again, ride in the panda car home, beating, name calling and utter despair.

Monday morning came and Dad refused to let me go to work. I spent the day lazily watching the world and my life slip by.

Monday night I was summoned downstairs.

'Mum's up the duff.'

Someone pushing me off a cliff couldn't have come as more of a surprise.

'Probably not mine, be someone else she's fucking about with got 'er like it.'

'Dick!' Mum looked hurt, I think, but then again he did have a point. What with Uncle Harry still visiting and Kenneth still on the scene, how could she be sure?

'Mum, you're 40.' I didn't know what else to say.

'I know but I don't look it.' She was right; she didn't. Considering the hard life she had lived, she could have looked a lot worse. At least her looks were better than her actions.

'Come on, you; we're going to the pub.' Dad was asking me to go to the pub! I didn't want to go; how dare he act like nothing had happened, the arsehole. I went; what was the point of another argument? I quite enjoyed the Rose and Crown. Dad sipped brandy and milk and I vodka and orange; no one seemed to care I was underage. If Dad had known what world he was opening up for me he would never have taken me; or would he?

It became a habit, going to the pub four or five times a week. After dinner, leaving Mum at home off we would go, not returning till closing time. Dad mellowed as the drink warmed his ice-ridden soul with every passing brandy. This allowed me to circulate, meet others, meet men.

By this time in my life I had no morals; I had given up trying to be anything more than what Dad said I was; what Mum and Dad had made me. Men gave me attention and I was back to the confusion of mixing lust, sex and love. I started sleeping with four or five different people, a mixture of men and boys, boys for the eye candy and men for the good times that the boys couldn't afford. I had become the whore my father had always accused me of being and predicted I would become.

'There's a letter for you.'

'Who, me?'

'Yes, you.' Mum's scornful look penetrated my so carefully crafted armour as she thrust the envelope toward my outstretched hand.

I looked at the child-like scrawl that decorated the small white envelope and wondered who it was from.

'Open it.'

I tore it open and pulled out the lined sheets haphazardly stuffed inside, scanning the words immediately.

'It's from Eddie.'

'Huh.' Mum huffed off, obviously in a mood.

Dear Anna, I know you are still angry with me but I cannot believe you won't answer any of my letters. (What letters? I thought.) I have been really ill in hospital and had time to think. I still love you and still want to marry you. Please phone me.

TLND Eddie xx

Eddie always signed his cards or letters TLND: True Love Never Dies.

I softened for a moment, but then the hurt returned disguised as anger. *Fuck him, let him rot*, I thought, but the voice inside cried.

I told Mum about the letter; she went to the drawer and grabbed a small bundle of opened letters all addressed to me, all from Eddie. She didn't even have the decency to explain why she not only kept them from me but also opened and read them, and I couldn't be bothered with listening to her trying to justify it.

I took the letters to my room and read them one by one. It turned out Eddie had deep vein thrombosis, his leg was bandaged top to bottom, he couldn't drive and had only just come out of hospital after a four-week stay. He was never one with words; the letters were short but told me all I needed to know. Checking my change I left the house to walk to the phone box.

Mum fussed and argued all morning; it was Sunday, and I had agreed to see Eddie to talk. His friend was bringing him down and they were staying to lunch.

When they arrived you would think it was royalty. Mum stuffed cushions behind Eddie's back, put his foot on a stool, ruffled his hair, all the time preening herself and giggling like a love-sick schoolgirl; it was pathetic. I sat and watched trying to dispel the thoughts of them naked together, intimate, his hands touching her like they had touched me. Briefly the fleeting memory of Kenneth lying on top of Mum whilst I looked through the window returned, a picture of her cold expressionless face watching me cry out to her popped into my mind: the same look she had given me when I went into the front room on the day I found out about her and Eddie; a victorious look. Where did they do it? Did he enjoy it? Had they ever done it again? It was clear Mum wanted to. Eddie watched me warily.

'Let's talk,' I said after lunch. Eddie couldn't make the stairs so we took over the front room whilst everyone sat in the kitchen; even Dad obliged, getting out of the way by going down the pub.

'Why?' My first question spilled the moment the room had emptied.

'Because she was crying; I felt sorry for her.'

'I feel sorry for the old boy next door since his wife died, doesn't mean I would fuck him.'

Eddie's eyes were downcast to the floor. His good foot fidgeted, wearing circles in the carpet.

'Did you enjoy it?'

He didn't answer.

'Well, did you?' The anger started to simmer like a pan over a low heat; tiny bubbles of rage came to the surface and popped in sounded words.

'Yes.'

'Well, she's had plenty of experience.'

'Don't.'

'Why not? Don't fucking protect her, she's my fucking mother for Christ's sake, and you, my ex-fiancé, had sex with her!'

'I know, I'm sorry, it was a mistake.' His voice was hardly audible, no match for my stifled anger.

I paced the floor firing questions at him as sharp as arrows, wanting to wound him, hurt him like he had hurt me; I hit the target every time, bringing him metaphorically to his knees.

Dad returned and demanded tea and telly. Our conversation ended abruptly before it was finished, so reluctantly I agreed that as soon as Eddie could drive he should come back alone and we would talk further.

147

After he left Mum was cool and distant. I had decided to bide my time until the right moment and confront her with the whole thing.

That moment came a few days later. It was the rare occasion of Dad actually going to work for the day. I sat at the kitchen table and watched her making tea.

'He told me.'

'Told you what?'

'About the two of you.'

'So?'

'What do you mean, "so"? He's my boyfriend, you're my mother!'

'He's not any more, is he?' She turned and looked at me, no expression registered. 'So what? It just happened, we had sex, he is lovely, you know I think that.'

'Stunned' is an understatement. A tsunami of rage, hurt and anger pent up for years burst through the dam of decency and flooded her with a torrent of abuse. Spent, tearstained and rasping for breath I laid my head on the table.

'You finished? He is nothing to you, you don't love him, never have. I don't see why you should marry Prince Charming when I am stuck with all this.' She waved her hand through the air. 'Why should you have it all? You don't know what I go through.'

'No, no I don't, but I know what I go through, and you're supposed to be my mum.'

'I protect you every day. If it wasn't for you I would have left long ago, but...'

Her voice tailed off into a wistful world.

'What do you mean?'

'Nothing, forget it.' She cut me dead; I knew there wasn't any point in going on, and I wasn't going to get resolution, because there was none to be had. I had two choices. Put the whole thing in the box of darkest memories and bury it deep inside with the rest of the shit or keep it alive and hurt every day. I chose the first.

Eddie visited a few weeks later. We talked into the night and there on the front room floor in front of the log fire we had make-up sex. As he spooned me from behind and pushed himself into me all I could picture was him and Mum. As he groaned his release with pleasure I groaned my anguish.

CHAPTER NINETEEN

What is the definition of grounding, laying down one's roots, dropping anchor? It I am sure holds a different meaning for each individual depending on what their teachings and experiences have been.

Moving home was not new to me, so moving again from country to town was just normality.

Nowadays I lay my roots and set anchor in self-belief and try to encourage all around me to do the same; after all, what is normal? What society expects? And if so precisely what is that? It is down to the individuals of society to ascertain what they find acceptable as normal, and that as I have said before is as unique to you as your fingerprint.

The move was inevitable. Mum's bump grew along with the pile of packed boxes. At least this time we had notice to quit so we didn't have the rush in the middle of the night.

A few weeks before we moved Dad's friend Andy came to stay for the weekend. I don't even know where or how Dad met him. I had certainly never seen him before then. He was a tall fair-haired man; at a guess I would judge him to be in his thirties.

Mum was about seven months pregnant; her cravings for sherbet fountains with a liquorice stick were insatiable, so when she asked me to go to the local shop to get her one I readily agreed, happy to do the mile or so walk in return for escape from the house. When Andy asked if I wanted company I readily agreed. I had seen his appreciative eyes running over my youthful figure; after all Mum was no challenge in her state. I don't know, maybe I thought this was payback time, something that I could have that she couldn't. I needed to reassure myself someone still wanted me, I needed to feel loved, desired. I had earned a reputation after being found out to be playing around with several of the locals at once; one by one they had lost interest. That in itself didn't bother me, I was bored with their attention anyway, none of them had satisfied the empty longing inside me. I was running wild. I had given up on all hope of ever being any different from Mum and Dad.

Andy and I walked in silence to the store but on the way back fell into flirty conversation. He grabbed my hand and spun me to kiss him. Excitement raged; the sensation thrilled me from my lips to all the right parts, setting off tingling muscle-clenching in my abdomen. It took little persuasion to get him to take me into the woodland that edged the lane. We fumbled clumsily into a position where his lips were on my neck and his hand cupped between my legs, forcing his fingers into me, finding my wetness. I loved it, the thought of the taboo sex meant he wanted me and only me. Just at the crucial moment of his zip undoing and his erection springing into the daylight I heard Dad's voice calling my name. We stumbled onto the road straightening our clothes. I held my chin high and defiant as I faced Dad. Andy wasn't so brave and tried to mutter the lame excuse of an injured rabbit. My head was filled with unspoken words. *There, you've always said I was a whore, are you happy, you're right.*

Dad said nothing until 'Mum's in labour. We need to get an ambulance quick.'

The next few hours were filled with worry. Mum was only seven months gone. Dad refused to go to the hospital; coward that he was he used me as an excuse, saying I was scared to be alone, he couldn't leave me. Andy had tactfully made rapid departure as soon as we had got back to the house, which left just me and Dad pacing the floor.

'Let's go to the pub,' he finally said.

'Don't you want to ring the hospital?'

'No, what for? The baby's probably dead anyway.'

'What about Mum?'

'Oh, she'll live. I'll ring in the morning.'

We went to the pub, Dad took pats on the back and played the big important father-to-be, free drinks took him to a state of oblivion. I eventually carried him home and laid him on the sofa.

Three days later I went with him to meet Mum and bring her home. I visited my tiny baby brother in intensive care, wired up to pipes and tubes, a shrivelled red minute individual fighting for his life, born into a world like mine. I sobbed. Dad wouldn't even see him. At the time I was angry but now as I reflect I think it was his self-preservation; he didn't think my little brother Gavin would survive so what was the point in bonding? No, he left Mum to cope alone.

Gavin was still in hospital when we moved some 30 or so miles to Swanley. Eddie was better so he helped us. We hadn't really got back together, just used each other really for casual sex. By now I knew I didn't love him; how could I? I didn't have a clue how to love anyone.

Two months later frail and small Gavin came home. That was the day I took the responsibility on myself to protect him against all odds. I was not going to let another brother die.

'I am so ill, I keep being sick, Mum, and I feel terrible.' No one was allowed to be ill in our house except Dad. His constant hypochondria had grown slowly worse over the years. Now we lived in a council house and got our rent paid by the social along with benefits and a stream of handouts from various charities, he didn't bother to work at all. He had no real pride.

'Don't tell your dad; he'll go mad if he thinks you've got something catching. Make yourself a doctor's appointment.' So I did.

The doctor tested everything, heart, blood pressure, temperature and urine; he told me to return if I was no better in a week but before the week was up I had a letter from the surgery asking me to go in.

I entered the sterile waiting room full of coughing spewing individuals; most people in those days were really unwell before they went to the doctor's! The matronly receptionist looked at me with her cool eyes and asked, 'Name?'

'Anna Carter.'

'You have no appointment booked.' She looked over the top of her glasses assessing what to do with me next.

'I have a letter,' I said, handing it to her.

'One moment, I will get your notes.'

I waited head of the queue forming behind me.

'Congratulations, Mrs Carter; it is positive.'

'What is?'

'Your test, you're expecting a baby.'

The beaming smile formed into a recoil of disgust when I replied, 'It's Miss Carter.'

I walked home with the words '*it's positive*' echoing in my ear. How could I be pregnant? We always used a condom, always... except for that one time. Realisation dawned on me: the make-up sex! But that was months ago. I tried to calculate my last period but couldn't remember. All I knew for sure was that I was 17, unmarried and pregnant and in 1977 that was still a mortal sin. I was terrified of everything but mostly what Dad would say.

Much ado about nothing, to coin a phrase; Dad was fine. He did ask who the father was and I dutifully answered, 'Eddie of course.' He was pleased, no name calling, no abuse, no nothing. I couldn't help wondering what the hell he was planning.

Eddie took it OK; his parents didn't. I was already 14 weeks when I found out about the baby. An abortion didn't even enter my mind until people started throwing the word around as a logical solution. It was how I found Eddie's weakness: his mother's whining. She filled his every waking moment with probing doubt, injecting poisonous thoughts through venomous fangs every time she bit another chunk out of his self-esteem. 'The baby's going to come out black you know, it's not yours, you'll see.' I sat and listened to her stoning him with rocks made from untruths until he could stand no more.

He never explained, or said goodbye, just left one day and never returned. I faced life as a future parent alone. After the tears as always came the hardness. I would succeed, I would be a good mum, I didn't know how but I would get out of this mess... the only worry on my horizon that I acknowledged was Gavin's welfare.

A few weeks before my son Darren was born Gavin pulled a cloth from the table; on the table was a jug of hot water containing a jar of baby food; he was hungry. It was a complete accident. The screaming filled the house from walls to ceilings, Mum's, mine and Gavin's mixed together in frenzied panic. Dad yelled at Mum for being a fucking stupid cow and leaving the jug where she did, she yelled back. They continued to argue as I dunked Gavin's legs and chest under cold running water.

'Get a fucking ambulance,' I yelled, breaking up their petty arguing. Sense kicked in and Mum ran to the call box whilst Dad stood as far away from us as possible and watched in silence.

'Who's coming to the hospital with us?' The ambulance men had done their best to calm Gavin's excruciating pain; his once-agonising screams had subsided to sobs; he now whimpered and trembled in Mum's arms.

'She can go.' Dad pointed at me.

'Dick, I'll go.' Mum stood up.

'No you won't, she can go. You need to be 'ere to cook my tea.' His harsh words cut deep; Mum knew she had her orders. I couldn't believe then and still don't understand now just how weak she was. I as most would walk a thousand miles over hot coals for my children, let alone miss one measly meal. 'I have to eat regular you see, I'm ill myself.' He directed the last sentence at the ambulance driver.

'I'll go, Mum.'

She handed Gavin into my outstretched arms. I cradled his fitfully sleeping body as gently as I could, trying to protect him against all the jolts and bumps of the journey until we arrived at Dartford hospital.

Gavin was treated and admitted to a ward. I sat beside his skinny frame that lay on a crisp white sheet, swathed in dressings, and watched his chest rise and fall as he slept. He was going to be fine, dressings and treatment for a few weeks; apparently he was lucky, though I don't know how.

'Mrs Carter.'

'Yes.' I was so used to midwives, hospitals and doctors calling me Mrs to save embarrassment in my delicate state, though whose embarrassment I am not sure, certainly not mine.

'Oh, another one so soon?' The woman facing me was young herself, maybe mid-twenties, her pale face furrowed with confusion as her eyes fixed on my bump.

'Oh, sorry, no, I'm not his mum, I'm his sister.'

'Tessa, duty social worker; mind if I ask some questions?' The woman's hand was held outstretched towards mine.

Tessa became part of our lives for quite a while. She was kind and thoughtful and Dad milked it for all he could get, food parcels, clothes, money, toys: some we kept, most were sold to get money for fags and drink. Previous records were incomplete so Tessa had little information on the past and instead judged her findings on what she saw and heard. I still didn't tell her things that were happening, not about selling the stuff she got for us, not about the times when Dad would put his face to Gavin's and yell so loud that my brother shook and silenced in fear, not about the rows, the smashing up of crockery and furniture that was so much a part of our daily life. No, I didn't want her interference, I had let other brothers die, this one I would protect, it was my duty not hers. Social workers had let me down once too often.

One warm morning on an early summer's day my son came into this world. After an induction and difficult birth I was wheeled into a side room once again to avoid embarrassment and given this 7lb 7oz baby boy that was all mine. I was only 17 but I felt no weight of responsibility, no worry; I had cared for others most of my life, what was one more?

Later that night a tentative knock on the door stirred me from an exhausted sleep. Eddie entered the room. He explained that Mum had got in touch and told him Darren was not black but in fact looked just like him. After arguing with his mum and dad he had come to see for himself. He held his tiny son and cried. Darren's dark eyes and brown hair reflected in the glassy image of Eddie's eyes their similarities.

Things snowballed, his parents came to visit and accepted Darren was in fact their grandson, Eddie asked me to marry him and without my even remembering saying yes the date was booked, I was home with Darren and Eddie moved in with us at Mum and Dad's.

CHAPTER TWENTY

What is the definition of true love? I certainly didn't know it at the age of 18 and I'm not even sure if I or anyone else knows it at all. If being with someone makes you happy, is that it? Love comes in many shapes and forms; I knew I didn't love Eddie in what I perceived then to be the true sense of the word but he was kind, generous, working, made me laugh and just had something about him. Was that enough to marry him? In hindsight probably not, but at the time it was not the only but definitely the best option and I truly thought that maybe, just maybe I would grow to love him.

Eddie moved in. We shared the front bedroom at Mum and Dad's three-bedroomed council house set on a much less than desirable estate on the outskirts of Kent close to where it bordered London.

At first everything seemed OK. I had put Eddie's confession behind me. Mum was still as flirty as ever but only when Dad wasn't around, but then that wasn't often and I knew Eddie, Darren and I wouldn't live there for long so I let it go over my head. Eddie changed his job and went to be a fork lift driver in a warehouse; he worked four nights a week, Monday through to Thursday. 'Less hours' work for more pay... more time to spend with you.' His optimism for the future glowed through his eyes and words.

Money-wise things were good. It was the seventies; few women knew what their men earned, me included, but I knew we had enough to dig us from this slimy dirt-ridden hole to a better lifestyle, enough to give our son Darren a better future.

Eddie was never a romantic man but he was kind and gentle, the complete opposite to Dad and that in itself was enough for me.

We had our wedding booked for 25 August. A few months before the big day, I left Eddie sleeping and took baby Darren shopping for a dress; though only eight weeks had passed since his birth I had worked hard at losing weight. I didn't want a wedding dress as such; the occasion was going to be small, we had all agreed. *Functional*, Eddie's mum had said; *serving a purpose*, added his dad. I kept quiet; after all, what else did I deserve?

Leaving Eddie sleeping after a long night shift I left behind the shadows of the house and took Darren into the warm summer sunshine.

I gazed at my reflection in the shop's full-length mirror. My breast heaved still full of milk under the thin cheesecloth material; I quite liked it. Until getting pregnant I had always been fairly flat-chested; Dad had made sure that I remembered this fact, often calling me 'titless' and 'like a bloke'. Now the mirror in front of me reflected back a slender but curvaceous young woman.

The shop assistant crooned compliments over how beautiful I looked; sales patter. Staring into my own blue-grey eyes the happiness of a bride-to-be was nowhere to be found. Moments ticked by as I stood listening to the shouting going on in my head. *Why are you doing this? You don't love this man. This is for life.* I silently argued back, *What's the alternative?* A whimper from the pram signalled Darren's opinion,

'I'll take it.' I wasn't going to let myself fall any further into doubt. I had to do this; it was for the best... for everyone.

On the way home the spring in my step faltered, the raging doubts poured torrents of reasons why I shouldn't carry this on... yet none seemed enough to drown my determination to rise from the stagnant past.

On my return the house was quiet, Mum and Dad were out and Eddie was still sleeping soundly. Just lately he had been harder and harder to wake, becoming grumpy and irritable. We put it down to the sheer exhaustion of having a new baby around. I was tired but it was my job to look after Darren, and I made sure that no one could accuse me of anything less than perfection.

With Darren fed, changed and sleeping peacefully in his pram, I tripped the stairs to our room, new dress in one hand and tea for Eddie in the other.

Curling up next to his warm body I shook him gently. 'Baby, it's time to wake up.' There was no response. It was another ten minutes or so before I eventually got him to respond.

'Fuck off and leave me alone.'

Wow, the force of his words shocked me. It wasn't what he said, I was used to that type of language and far worse; it was the fact that he was so aggressive, a side of him I had never seen or heard before.

'Hey, come on, I know you're tired but you've got to get up for work.'

'I said FUCK OFF.' A hard shove accompanied his words.

Falling off the bed I let out an involuntary shout. The noise fuelled his anger. The blind rage that followed left me stunned. Catapulting out of the bed he dragged me to my feet before slapping my face hard enough to knock me back down from where I had just been lifted.

'Fuck off.' He was barely awake, that usual face full of softness replaced by a hard clenched jaw, glowering at me with a fire of rage reflected in his unrecognisable expression.

159

I fled the room quicker than the tears that coursed down my fast-swelling face.

Shaking I ran downstairs. Standing in the middle of the empty kitchen, gasping sobs racking my body, I tried to compose myself, still reeling from the shock. I held my face as I rinsed my mouth with cold water that spat out red into the sink, splashing bloody polka dots onto the white porcelain. What the hell had just happened?

By the time Mum and Dad returned I was sat in the front room gingerly sipping tea.

'You OK?' Mum was no doubt taken aback by the state of me. She stood awkwardly, knowing my answer surely should have bought compassion but it was as if she didn't know what to do.

'What you done now?' Dad's voice was matter-of-fact.

'He hit me, Eddie hit me.' I sobbed uncontrollably, overcome by the reality of what had happened.

'Must have deserved it.'

I knew Dad would say something like that, how could he say anything else, it was in his make-up.

'I just tried to wake him up.'

I looked at the crumpled dress thrown on the sofa; Mum's eyes followed mine.

'Oh, you've got a dress then?'

Were these people in another world? Did they not hear what I just said? Had they not taken in the state I was in?

I sat in silence.

'Don't just stand there, Barb; make the fucking tea.' Dad sat in his chair and lit up a cigarette. The moment was over, brushed under the carpet without a second thought.

I left Eddie to sleep, too scared to wake him; he was late for work. When he woke and came down the stairs his concern for me was genuine.

'Why didn't you wake me? I'm late now.' He looked at me. 'Christ, Anna, what the hell happened?' In a split second he had crossed the room and fell to his knees cradling my chin in his hands, inspecting the eye that was now swollen and angry. He traced his finger down the purple-blue haze that ran like a brush mark from cheekbone to chin. 'What happened?' he repeated.

'Nothing, nothing, I'm fine.' I dropped my chin, unable to look into the eyes of a man I had trusted. Eddie shot a stabbing look at Dad, though Dad didn't see. I knew at that moment that Eddie was either a very good liar or he genuinely didn't remember hitting me; which was yet to be proven.

The next morning Eddie returned from work. Darren had, as new babies do, had a restless wakeful night. I was exhausted and glad that he had now decided to sleep. Eddie slipped into bed beside me, pressing his eager nakedness into my back. My body may have been warm but my reception was icy cold.

'What's wrong?' he asked. 'Tell me what happened to you.' He tried to snuggle close but I moved to the edge of the bed. Eventually with persuasion I turned to face him and there, with my hand tucked under my head, rested up on my elbow and looked into his deep brown eyes. Was this all real? Had this happened? It was hard to believe now, lying here with him, feeling so safe and warm. I brought my hand to my face, pressing the bruise to remind me of the pain; I winced.

'You hit me.' The words were out, suspended in the silence on a gossamer thread spun from fear. I continued to explain whilst he protested his innocence. In the end the conversation was left with him truly believing I was covering for Dad and using him as a scapegoat. How the hell he could reason that conclusion I don't know, but he did.

Life moved on. I became wary of waking Eddie, or even disagreeing with him. The effect on my health was obvious as the weight fell from me.

'Too much sex, cock-sucking isn't food you know.' Dad's crudity was full of concern. He actually seemed worried, as did Mum. Was this out-of-character behaviour real caring or was there an underlying reason? I had become a pessimist, always looking for the bad stuff, but then if that was what was normal to receive was I really pessimistic or just realistic?

Dad got a job in a paper factory. For the few short weeks leading up to the wedding he seemed content. He was out of the house a lot which left me in peace. Eddie's parents decided that my family had no idea how to organise a wedding so, as they wanted to keep it as small and out of the public eye as possible, they took over all arrangements. They decided no photographer or flowers were needed, just a few very close family on their side, my mum, my dad and Gavin. A reception of sorts was to follow, held at their house with a few selected guests, not including my parents. I let them arrange everything; what was the point in fighting? Just for once I wanted a peaceful life.

Eddie planned two weeks off work, one before the wedding and one after. It was in the week before the wedding that what happened should have once and for all changed my mind. As you read on you will no doubt question my strength and sanity but what you have to take into consideration is that I had 18 years of abuse tucked firmly under my belt before this week. I don't know but maybe by then I had just run out of fight.

Dad was working, Darren and Gavin were sleeping. It was a Friday afternoon. We all knew Dad would go straight from work to the pub. A cash-paid weekly wage gave him the justification to do this. I remember his words, always the same every Friday when he came home slurring; falling into the front room he would say three things in this order.

'What, ain't a working man entitled to a drink with his friends after a long hard week?' This statement would be followed by a string of abuse thrown haphazardly into space to be caught by any ears present.

Secondly he would ask where his dinner was. After calling his dinner shit and throwing it across the room, usually aimed at but missing Mum, he would then demand a mug of tea. On a light-hearted note I think more money was spent in our house on replacement crockery than on food and bills put together. Maybe that's why now Mum is so fussy about having everything nice and matching.

This Friday afternoon Eddie went for a lie down; so did Mum. I stayed up to clear away and prepare dinner, promising Eddie I would join him shortly.

When all was done I kept my promise and tiptoed lightly up the stairs. I pushed the closed door of our room softly so as not to wake Darren who shared a room with us.

The room was bathed in muted sunlight dimmed by the thin closed curtains. Eddie lay on top of the covers, stripped naked, one arm tucked behind his head, the other round Mum who was also naked.

I stood frozen to the spot. 'What the fuck is going on?' I was rooted, unable to move. The seconds that seemed like eternity bound my lips and breathing. I tried to still my racing heart but the blood pounded relentlessly in my ears, a roaring that threatened to overwhelm my consciousness.

'Come and join us, it will be fun.' Eddie purred like a contented lion. Mum turned toward him, wrapping her leg over his nakedness. Her smile was that of a stranger, or was it? No, I had seen this smile before, way back.

'Do it.' Eddie's voice was hard, cold and harsh. The order he gave shot me, a bullet of deceit fired from the gun of an unfaithful and perverse individual.

The noise of a key scrabbling to find a lock filtered through my incomprehension of the scene before me. Everything happened so fast. Things changed in an instant but the subliminal message stayed embossed on my mind so deep that even to this day I can close my eyes and relive the minutes I stood looking on.

'Fuck, it's Dick, he's early.'

Mum dragged her clothes from the floor into her scrambling hands. Eddie dived under the duvet, aiming orders for me to get in beside him. I pulled the covers up to my chin just in case Dad looked in and saw I was fully dressed, he might get suspicious... what the hell was I thinking? I should be out there ranting and shouting about what had just happened. What was the point? Dad wouldn't believe me and even if he did it would still end up as my fault.

Eddie stilled; we lay there listening to the argument.

'You fucking lazy cow, lying in bed whilst I work my bollocks off to keep this house in order. I suppose you had your fancy man mauling you whilst I've been working, you slut. Get out of the bed and make me some fucking dinner.' The bang that followed told me Dad had tipped the bed to get Mum up. I had no sympathy, she was a slut, but what did that make Eddie or in fact me?

This happened exactly one week before the wedding yet I continued as planned, blocking the event from my mind and burying it with all the rest of the stuff that was festering inside me waiting to poison me to destruction.

CHAPTER TWENTY-ONE

25 August dawned. By 7 am it was already warm, the morning of the day bringing with it a misty start that carried the promise of a hot day ahead. I stretched out in my bed, turned to lie on my back and let out a deep sigh. I should have been elated or at least excited. I should have been nervous, giggly, woken up by Mum or a gaggle of flapping bridesmaids desperate to crack the champagne. That's what happens on your wedding day, isn't it? It's what happened on my daughter's.

But there was I lying staring at the ceiling, listening to the stillness of the room broken only by the occasional snuffle from Darren, lying peacefully sleeping in his cot, and the chatter of nature floating on the soft breeze that fanned the net curtain as it flowed through the open window.

The enormity of the day that lay ahead swamped me; the air in the room stifled the intake of my breathing. I had no excitement, no enthusiasm, none of the trimmings a woman is led to expect on the morning of her wedding. There was just nothing. I now look on that day and realise what I was feeling that morning was acceptance, acceptance of what was to be, recognition and resignation to fate. In a way I had given up; all those years of survival and striving to overcome the physical, mental and sexual abuse I had received had led to me accepting my fate as written in the stars, out of my control.

Eddie had stayed the night at his parents': nothing to do with the usual superstition that it was unlucky to see the bride on the night before, no, just convenience. His parents lived a short car journey from Woolwich registry office, where we were getting married. I can't remember much about the wedding, not even how I got there; strange because although I have now been re-married 23 years, I can remember that wedding with clarity. Perhaps that's the difference being in love makes? Though my memories of marrying Eddie are sketchy I have photos that someone, although I don't remember who, took of the day. They show a solemn-faced frowning groom standing with his new bride; she or should I say I wore a cheesecloth dress, open-toed sandals and a fixed smile.

Wedded bliss? There was no honeymoon; that night we returned to Mum and Dad's. They hadn't come to the reception; they hadn't been invited, but even if they were I am sure they wouldn't have come. Mum would have wanted to, a chance to socialise, flirt and let her hair down, but Dad would never have allowed it. We arrived home late, creeping into the house so not to wake anyone, but Dad was waiting. His voice bellowed from above, '*Fucking shut the noise*'; the words fell over each other, bowled for us to catch. Conscious that this was the potential beginning of an onslaught I did the best I could not to aggravate the situation further. We quietly tiptoed to bed and lay in silence; no wedding night sex for us. I had made my marital bed and now I was well and truly lying in it.

All returned to normal on the following Monday; apart from the gold band adorning the third finger of my left hand there was no evidence of the wedding ever happening.

We only stayed at Mum and Dad's a few weeks. We found a little two-bed house in the next street. It took all the money we had or should I say Eddie had, costing a little under £6000, leaving us little if any money for furniture and stuff. By begging and borrowing and with a few gifts we managed the sparse necessities and planned to move in at the end of September.

In the few weeks before we left Mum and Dad's Eddie became moody and short-tempered. He paid no attention to Darren, calling him a screaming brat. I was tired to the extent of exhaustion; my patience and temper ran on a fine thread suspended between reality and fantasy. We rowed constantly, just as Mum and Dad did. The house was a war zone. Darren sensed the atmosphere and became more and more fretful and demanding; I began for the first time to resent his intrusion in my life. I felt trapped, imprisoned and helpless.

The day finally came when the three of us moved into our own house. Again you would think that would be a memory I would hold, but I cannot recall it at all. All that had held me together throughout those weeks was the hope that once we were living in our own home things would improve. Oh, how very wrong I was.

I hated the nights when Eddie worked; Monday to Thursday from six in the evening till nine the next morning Darren and I were alone. It doesn't sound long, after all most of the time is sleeping time, but I hated it. Caught between the devil and the deep blue sea, the lesser of two evils, many nights I would pack up a bag and return to sleep at Mum and Dad's to escape the nightmare of being alone.

I couldn't really cook. I tried but no one had ever shown me; I had picked up the little knowledge I had myself. It goes without saying we lived on a diet that consisted largely of Smash instant mash, baked beans, fish fingers and artic roll for desert on Sundays. Understandably Eddie often suggested we go to his parents' for dinner; after all there was no point in them coming to ours! It became the norm for us to go shopping on a Monday, then to his parents' for dinner before going home and Eddie going off to work.

November came, frosty and cold; excitement buzzed in me like an overactive bee. This was to be our first Christmas as a family.

'Let's go Christmas shopping,' Eddie suggested; I couldn't wait.

We trailed round the shops, mingling in the crowds; to all intents and purposes we were a normal happy young family, and we were... Apart from the angry outbursts from Eddie that had grown more frequent, the past had faded into the distance, blinded by coloured lights and carol singers. I was happy.

We returned home exhausted with arms full of gifts. Eddie had bought me the *Grease* album and I him tiger-skin seat covers for his new car. I wanted to wrap our gifts for each other but he was too excited and went straight out to put the covers on the car seats whilst I put Darren down for an afternoon sleep.

When Eddie came in I was in the kitchen preparing dinner. 'Coffee?' I asked. He nodded as he rested lazily against the work surface. I filled the kettle; the tap hissed nosily as it splashed water into the metal. As I turned the tap off the hissing quietened, replaced by a similar sound I found vaguely familiar.

'Eddie, I can hear your heart beating.'

'I'm fine,' he replied as he rubbed his chest.

'Let me listen.' I moved toward him.

'Get off me.' His voice was followed with a shove that sent me stumbling across the kitchen. Fear flowed through my veins, cascading, overflowing, but was quickly replaced by anger. *How fucking dare he? I was only worried.*

'Fuck you,' I screamed, trying to regain my balance and composure. Darren's scream pierced the air, wiping out the words Eddie yelled. I bounded upstairs. Picking up Darren I turned to find Eddie right behind me; his eyes glowed, fired with anger. He went to strike out. Deep within me flooded the memory of Dad attacking me whilst I held Carl in my arms and I was that child again, only I knew this time I had to escape. Diving under his swinging arm I gripped Darren tightly to my chest. I had no plan; I just knew I had to get out of the house. Eddie's heavy footsteps pounded behind me as I raced down the stairs, and then silence; in slow motion I lifted my body from the hallway floor. Eddie had pushed me; I had tumbled, my whole weight landing on Darren; he was limp, eyes closed... Another piercing scream ripped through the air... only this time it was mine.

The hospital light reflected stark and white, the same pale hue as my skin. Eddie sat in silence wringing his hands in his lap. I couldn't bring myself to look at him let alone speak.

A social worker questioned us. *She fell on the stairs*, Eddie said. I agreed. I wanted to say, *You pushed me!* But social workers were the last people I wanted on my case; my life had seen enough. All I wanted was a safe happy childhood for my son who was now lying in hospital with a hairline fracture of the skull.

We sat beside him, Eddie and me, watching his tiny chest rise and fall as he slept. The doctors had left us with the reassurance he was going to recover and would be fine; they all accepted it as an accident, just one of those things, no one to blame. I did it, managed to keep quiet, managed to cover up the truth.

'Why, Eddie? Why did you do it?' I was all cried out my red eyes scanned his paleness.

'Do what?'

'This.' I cast my eyes towards Darren. 'Why did you lose it?'

'What the hell are you talking about?'

'You pushed me knowing I had Darren in my arms. Fucking hell Eddie, take your temper out on someone your own size, hit me if you must but...' I turned again to look at Darren and the tears began to fall, freshening the streaks already adorning my ashen face. 'Not your son, not your son.'

'I don't know what you mean? I heard you fall and came to see if you were all right.'

'FUCK DID YOU,' I spat angrily, looking him straight in the eye. And there it was: complete confusion, a pool of emptiness. 'You don't remember, do you?' He shook his head slowly, and I knew he was telling the truth. I couldn't forgive him for what he had done, but if he truly didn't remember how could I blame him? We talked long into the night; I told him exactly what had happened; he sobbed as I held him cradling his head against my chest, a lonely man, not much more than a boy, terrified of what was happening.

A week or so later Darren came home and the house returned to as near normal as possible. I was still wary but had talked Eddie into going to the doctor's, so felt a little more secure. Eddie trod on eggshells, being loving and gentle to us both, showering us with out-of-character affection.

The doctor put Eddie's episodes down to migraine; he had had a lot of headaches, especially recently. We put it down to stress and lack of sleep. The doctor gave him tablets and told him apart from that everything was fine.

On 1 December we put up our tree, switched on the lights and made love on the lounge floor. Since Eddie had been taking the tablets he had felt much better; a bout of sickness had laid him off work but that was all. His behaviour had mellowed to the gentle giant of a man I had known before and tried to love. I did still care very deeply for this man yet love escaped me; I wanted to love him, but what was love? Did I just have some fairy-tale unrealistic expectations? Eddie was good to us, food on the table, bills paid, a nice stable home and yet... was this enough? I decided it was and I was determined to be the best wife I could.

On 4 December, a Monday, we went shopping as usual and then to Eddie's parents. His dad was at work. Over the past few months his mum had mellowed; she absolutely doted on Darren and really, though it sounds awful, he was my inroad to acceptance by the family.

We had lunch with his mum. Jess the dog who idolised Eddie curled up at the base of the armchair where he sat splayed and relaxed. I shared the space with Jess, sitting on the floor resting my head on Eddie's knee; he stroked my hair. Darren slept soundly in the carry cot on the sofa with his granny next to him. Christmas programmes had started; our conversation was light. We were watching women's wrestling, which Eddie found hilarious; his laughter filled the cosy room. It was like a scene from a Christmas card, the family including the dog sat round the fire, the tree with its lights on twinkling in the corner, a perfect picture.

'We should go, it's three o'clock now and we've got to get back for you to get ready for work.'

'Yes, I suppose you're right; come on.' Eddie stretched lazily, arms above his head, and let out a contented sigh. Gathering our things we made to the hall.

'You know what? I think we will have another cuppa before we go.'

'But we're ready,' I said with my hand on the front door lock.

'No, no, I want another cuppa.' With that he turned and went back to the front room and plonked heavily into the same chair.

I can't say I wasn't a bit irritated, us staying any longer meant I didn't get any time with Eddie before he had to hurry off to work, but I dutifully made the tea and curled up on the floor next to the armchair.

Eddie leant forward and kissed the top of my head; my annoyance melted as a smile spread across my lips. Turning my face toward him he gripped my chin, hard.

171

'No matter what happens you know I will always love you.'

Eddie never said things like that in public, but surprise didn't have a chance to register. Within seconds he stiffened and threw his body back against the chair, let out a sigh and it was over.

The rest? I don't really remember. Hysteria, yes, shouting his name, yes, calling 999, yes, but that's all.

Eddie had suffered a massive heart attack; he died instantly. The post mortem showed he had a hole in the heart that had probably been there since birth; he also had hardening of his arteries.

My Eddie was dead, I was alone with Darren; what the hell was I going to do apart from fall apart?

CHAPTER TWENTY-TWO

The funeral came and went; my memory though vivid is also shrouded in the mist of grief. I was in the main car, chief mourner. The song *Forever Autumn* sung by Justin Hayward accompanied the coffin to its final destination.

I have regrets, regrets like everyone else; I had no idea Eddie was ill, let alone going to die. I say I wish we had known, but really do I? I say things would have been different, but would they? Would I have really wanted them to be? The years we had were definitely not perfect, in fact totally the opposite, but Eddie lived his life to the full, how he wanted, without being in fear of his final breath and that I wouldn't change.

Eddie's parents naturally were beside themselves with grief; after the funeral his mum became obsessed with seeing a medium and was convinced not only that Eddie was still in the house but that Darren was hers and she fought me tooth and nail for custodial rights. She lost. The bitterness that raged between us was never resolved and to this day I have never spoken to her or set eyes on her again. Darren still keeps in touch.

Love comes in many forms. Throughout this story I have said I didn't love Eddie and in truth I didn't; well, not in the way that constitutes marriage. But there was a longing for him, a respect, a sort of trust and a definite gratitude that he had in some ways, not all good, opened my eyes to reality and saved me.

After the initial shock of losing Eddie I realised I was about to become quite financially comfortable, what with insurance policies and the house along with his work's benefits, widow's allowance and a brand new car. I had money but I had no one to turn to for advice, just a well-stocked bank account.

It wasn't long before the panic attacks started; this time they raged uncontrollably. At night I would pace the floor robbed of sleep, sure that Eddie's ghost would appear, positive I was going to die, convincing myself that I had been left with a bad heart after the fire but no one had noticed. Palpitations raged, banging an out-of-rhythm beat alien to my chest. I would claw the windows gasping for breath. I was sure every second was to be my last.

Confused, beyond logical thinking I decided to get rid of the house and moved in with Mum and Dad; both of them had been trying to get me to move back since the day after the funeral. They said it was in my best interest, they could look after Darren and me, get us back on our feet. I believed them, but what really contributed to me making up my mind was that Eddie's parents stripped everything from the house before I sold it, taking every trace that we as a married couple ever existed. The reason they said was that they had their son for 21 years; I had had him a matter of months so they were more entitled than I to his possessions.

Moving in with Mum and Dad took me on roads I should never have travelled. My days were spent drinking away not only the grief of the past few months but the heartache of most of my life. My money dwindled fast.

Under a mixture of tranquilisers and whiskey with persuasion I married one of Dad's friends, had two more children, blew my fortune, attempted suicide, divorced, and turned into a sex and drug addict.

It took ten years to even start my road to recovery. It took a further ten years to achieve what I see as living rather than existing... But all that is another story...

END

PRETTY LITTLE GIRL

You are such a pretty little girl.
Don't pull back, I won't bite.

You are such a pretty, pretty little girl.

Shhh… don't talk,
Pretty girls don't need to talk.

You just sit and smile, and behave,
And look pretty.

Oh my pretty one
My how you have grown.

Don't pull away, come sit,
It's just a bit of fun.
My pretty, pretty girl.

Look at you…

Why are those boys looking at you?
What did you say?
What did you do?

Nothing but trouble
You pretty girl.

You stay here,
You can't leave me pretty one.

What would they want
With you?
You silly little thing,
What are you good for?

Nothing… but pretty